# 101 ways
## TO ADJUST TO
## HIGH SCHOOL

by Randy Howe

 PUBLISHING

NEW YORK

*Dedicated to the students and staff at The Sound School.*

This publication is designed to provide accurate and authoritative information in regard to the subject matter covered. It is sold with the understanding that the publisher is not engaged in rendering legal, accounting, or other professional service. If legal advice or other expert assistance is required, the services of a competent professional should be sought.

Editorial Director: Jennifer Farthing
Editor: Cynthia Ierardo
Production Editor: Caitlin Ostrow, Julio Espin
Production Artist: Todd Bowman
Creative Director: Lucy Jenkins
Cover Designer: Carly Schnur

Published by Kaplan Publishing, a division of Kaplan, Inc.
888 Seventh Ave.
New York, NY 10106

Printed in the United States of America

May 2007
07 08 10 9 8 7 6 5 4 3 2 1

ISBN-13: 978-1-4195-4177-3
ISBN-10: 1-4195-4177-3

Kaplan Publishing books are available at special quantity discounts to use for sales promotions, employee premiums, or educational purposes. Please email our Special Sales Department to order or for more information at *kaplanpublishing@kaplan.com,* or write to Kaplan Publishing, 888 7th Avenue, 22nd Floor, NY, NY 10106.

# INTRODUCTION

The truth is, it isn't *that* hard to adjust to high school, as long as you have a plan. This book will give you that plan. *101 Ways to Adjust to High School* is a source of information and inspiration. Its tips were provided by students, guidance counselors, and teachers from across the country. They will help to improve your high school experience.

Maybe you picked up this book for yourself, but chances are somebody got it for you, the reason being that everyone remembers how stressful high school can be. It isn't easy to balance a social life and schoolwork. It's tough to be studious when you have distractions like parties and movies and sports and jobs, and it's tough to enjoy those distractions when you're behind in your work. Then there are the ups and downs you will experience with friends and family. How are you supposed to find happiness while also giving your schoolwork the attention it deserves? Start by reading this book!

At this very moment you are going through the most important transition of your life, from childhood to adulthood. You're going from being dependent on grown-ups—like your parents and teachers—to a position of independence, which is a necessary change as you prepare for your next step, be it college, the military, or a full-time job. But let's not get ahead of ourselves.

```
Transition (noun):
```
A period of change.

Happiness comes from success and success in high school begins with a good report card, so be ready to put a lot of effort into your schoolwork. The good news is, a little bit of effort actually goes a long way. For example, there are a number of ways for you to raise your grade from a B− to a B+, which will improve your overall grade point average. By earning just five more points on a test, mission accomplished. By turning in just one extra-credit assignment, mission accomplished. By raising your hand at least once a day to ask a question or make a comment, and therefore boosting your class participation grade, mission accomplished! Success isn't just about working hard; it's also about working smart. If you are organized and if you follow the advice of former students, you can avoid the pitfalls of high school and receive report cards with a smile. You can even have a social life worthy of a fun-loving student like you! The point is this: your high school experience is something to be treasured rather than endured.

Whether you're an 8th grader, a student enjoying the summer before high school, or a current high school student who simply wants some help, this book is chock-full of helpful tips just for you. It won't take long to read and if you learn just one thing, then your time will be well worth it. Maybe you'll start using a calendar to keep track of important due dates. Maybe you'll cut back on how many hours you work, or socialize, or spend on extracurricular activities like sports and clubs, so you can spend more time on your studies. Maybe you'll start to ask Mom and Dad for help, considering they were once high school students too. This book isn't just about schoolwork, though. It's about forming healthy friendships and becoming the kind of person you want to be. It's about finding the kind of balance that allows you to have a good time while also being productive.

First, you will read about some of the things you can do before starting high school. Then, you'll find advice for those first few crazy, stressful, unforgettable days of 9th grade. By the way, we recommend that you read these pages even if you've already gone through 9th grade. The advice, for example, about making a good first impression, about what you should read during summer vacation, and about picking up the necessary school supplies is still relevant, after all, no matter what grade you're in. The next section provides general academic advice. The final sections touch on important aspects of your life, from family and friends to extracurricular activities and planning for the future, all of which is important if your teen years are to be a happy and successful.

Because students, teachers, and guidance counselors from all over the country contributed to this book, you can feel confident knowing that somebody from your neck of the woods, somebody who has some idea what your school is like, sent in tips. This is a book about you and for you. So rather than stressing out during your four years of high school, enjoy them as you should enjoy this book. Thank you for making *101 Ways to Adjust to High School* a part of your plan for success, and best of luck to you!

# Academics: Before school starts.

# Take classes for high school credit.

Believe it or not, you don't have to wait until 9th grade for your high school experience to begin . . .

### Top Three Reasons to Take Middle School Classes for High School Credit:

1. You will find out what a high school class is really like, from the difficulty of the work to the style of the teaching.

2. You will be able to take electives (optional classes of your own choosing) as a junior and senior because you'll have already completed your required classes.

3. As a senior, you might be able to leave school before dismissal (to work or participate in an internship) or even graduate early.

## "But which classes should I take?"

- **Pre-algebra**—if you have a tough time with math.
- **Algebra**—if you like math and want to be ahead of the game.
- **Biology or Earth/Life Science**—if you're a science whiz and want to take physics or an Advanced Placement (AP) science class as a junior or senior. (AP classes can earn you college credit while you're still in high school!)
- **Foreign language**—if you want to complete Spanish I before 9th grade and eventually take AP Spanish. (Most of our contributors recommend taking Spanish because it's a little more useful than French these days!)
- **Keyboarding**—if you want to write essays and papers without spraining a finger!
- **Composition**—if you want to improve your writing skills for schoolwork and standardized tests.
- **Study skills**—if you need help getting organized and staying organized; a good class will also help you to be more efficient in your efforts.

## Be an AVID Student!

*In California, there are "survival skills" classes called AVID (Advancement Via Independent Determination) to assist strug-gling students. These are usually a part of the regular day in middle school. If you are struggling in school, ask if there is a similar program available; don't wait until it's too late!*

# Ask the experts!
## Part 1: Teachers and guidance counselors.

It is a good idea to have a sit-down with a teacher or two, not to mention your guidance counselor, before graduating from middle school. By sit-down, we mean that you have a conversation rather than a spontaneous exchange in the middle of a crowded hallway between lunch and your next class! You want their undivided attention, and you want to be able to give your undivided attention.

Your priority should be to ask these folks what the major differences are between middle school and high school:

**1.** Is the scheduling different (seven or eight periods versus block scheduling)?

**2.** Do they "weight" classes, awarding more points in the class ranking to honors and AP classes?

**3.** Do they still rank students at graduation?

**4.** Will the class sizes be much bigger?

**5.** Will there be midterm exams in addition to quarterly exams and final exams?

**6.** What statewide tests will you have to take?

You'll also want to ask them to recommend the better teachers and guidance counselors. Some schools do allow their students to change classes and counselors.

# Ask the experts!
## Part 2: Current high school students.

After you have asked the adults which teachers are the best, you should find out from an upperclassman which teachers are the toughest and the easiest. Or maybe you'll settle for just knowing which ones are the nicest.

You might be curious about the food, so ask which meals are the best and the worst. Also, does everyone buy lunch?

Before wrapping up this sit-down, don't be afraid to ask the experienced high schooler to be serious for a minute. Ask them what they struggled with as freshmen and how you can avoid such problems. Believe it or not, they will be willing to share.

```
Upperclassmen (noun):
Juniors and seniors; some will
look down their noses at freshmen!
```

# Shadow a high schooler.

To "shadow" someone is to follow them closely, like a detective in a movie. In this case, you won't be shadowing a suspect; you'll be shadowing a student. To be specific, a high school student at a school you are deciding whether or not to attend.

The chance to shadow is often offered in the winter or spring of 8th grade. Prospective students are invited to take a tour and then go to a class or two with a student.

Although shadowing is an opportunity most often found in independent schools, nowadays many public schools (especially charter and magnet schools) are doing it too. This is their way of making sure that students go to a high school where they can be happy and successful. It's also a great way to learn where things are in the school and to meet a few people.

## Are You "Drawn" to Magnet Schools?

*A magnet school usually has a specific theme that attracts (thus the name "magnet") students from surrounding school districts. Acceptance is based on a lottery system. The same is true of charter schools, which tend to have different rules, schedules, and expectations than the typical high school.*

# Read!

If you wanted to get in shape, you'd work out a lot and eat healthy, right? To get your brain in shape for high school, think of magazines as fruits and vegetables, newspapers as running shoes, and books as free weights!

## "All right, all right, all right. I'll read! But what kinds of things should I read?"

NONFICTION (true) books are the best practice, as the majority of the reading for your classes will be of this type.

- Read autobiographies, also called memoirs, if you want to learn about incredible, real-life people. It's reality TV, library-style!

- Biographies tell about people, but from an outside perspective, which usually means these books are a bit more truthful and reliable.

- Newspapers and magazines will keep you up-to-date with current affairs (which usually comes in handy in at least one class). Even pop culture (music, fashion, gossip) magazines will exercise your mind.

- Blogs have a little more substance than e-mails and text messages and can be yet another source of valuable knowledge, depending on who's writing them—and who's responding to them!

- The school district's Web site offers a bit of reading, not to mention insight into things that will be affecting you, come September.

FICTION is an entertaining way to keep your brain in shape. There's a type for every taste:

- Mysteries
- Horror
- Romance
- Survival stories
- Sports-based novels
- Science fiction and fantasy
- Literary fiction (more serious, containing inference, irony, and intellectual intensity!)
- Graphic novels (also known as comic books)

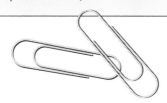

# Go to summer camp!
## Be more independent.

You might think that there's no connection between **avoiding bug bites** and avoiding bad grades, but there is. When Mom and Dad aren't around to remind you about insect repellant, you will either **remember to apply it** or be eaten alive! So remember that just as itchy mosquitoes make for a miserable summer, failing grades make for a miserable school year.

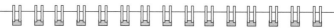

# Top Five Benefits of Spending the Summer at Camp:

1. It's fun!

2. You are your own person making your own decisions: about following camp rules, about who your friends are, and about what to spend your money on at the camp store or during field trips to town.

3. You will be able to try some things you've never tried before (spin art, the oboe, whatever), and this could give you reason to try other things in high school.

4. You will have the opportunity to make new friends, which could give you confidence to make new friends in high school.

5. Your parents will miss you and appreciate you when you come back home!

# Attend freshman orientation.

What was once just a trend at colleges and universities has now become popular with high schools. Whether freshman orientation to the high school is a three-day affair filled with a variety of events and experiences or just an afternoon taking a tour and getting your student ID, we highly recommend you attend yours.

Keep your ears open for the date, because some schools will offer their orientation in the spring of 8th grade, while others do it during the summer before 9th. And be sure to take the tour. You can't get where you need to be if you don't know where you need to go!

## Where's Your Map?

*Rather than letting your map of the school float around in your backpack like a fish in an aquarium, may we suggest you three-hole punch it and then put it in your binder? At some point, you won't need it anymore, but for those first few weeks, you'll want to keep it close at hand.*

# Get your locker in a hot spot.

Consider yourself lucky if your school allows you to pick your own locker, and then consider yourself wise if you get it in a "hot spot."

## Hot Spot Checklist:

 Close to the majority of classes, which will decrease the chances of your being late to class.

Near your friends, which means more fun during the good times and help to get through the hard times.
> NOTE: Be near your friends but do not share with your friends. Two people sharing one locker is an organizational nightmare and may even lead to an argument.

 If you get stuck in a cold spot—meaning far away from your friends and classes—you will feel isolated. Do all that you can to be near the main flow of things.

**Q:** "What kind of lock should I get?"

**A:** *Students recommend a combination lock. If you forget the combo, you can just check the slip that came with the lock when you bought it. (Keep this in your house.) If you get a lock that opens with a key and you lose that key, the custodian will have to cut your lock off, and you'll be out some cash.*

## The First Thing You Should Put in Your Locker

*A product search on Google turned up 20 "school locker organizers." Once you've got your locker, you might want to buy one of these to help keep you from desperately scrambling through all your things before each class. If not on the Internet, then get one at any office supply store.*

# Go on a shopping spree!

Of course, you've been doing back-to-school shopping for years, but there are some differences now that you're in high school. First and foremost is the level of responsibility you now have. In order to keep track of your things and your assignments, you will have to be very prepared and very well organized. In middle school, a sympathetic teacher might give you a binder or some paper; that might not be the case in high school.

## Top Ten School Supplies:

1. A 1.5-inch binder with dividers for each class, and a clear plastic cover sheet so that you can slip your schedule (and map of the campus) inside it for those first few days

2. A "binder reminder" assignment book, which can be secured into your binder

3. Pencils, pens, and multicolored highlighters

4. Lined paper, three-hole punched, for your binder

5. A couple of pads to use as scrap paper (not for class notes—those go on the paper that's already in your binder)

6. Yellow sticky pads for reminders

7. A stapler, staples, and paper clips (multicolored paper clips help with organization)

8. A three-hole punch, if it fits in your binder, or a single-hole punch, so that you can put papers into your binder right after the teacher hands them to you

9. If it doesn't cost too much, an electronic "binder reminder" like a personal digital assistant (PDA) can be very beneficial (In addition to keeping track of important addresses and phone numbers, you will also have a daily calendar at your fingertips)

10. Discs or a jump drive to bring information from the computer lab at school to your computer at home

# Look for activities that begin *before* school starts.

When talking to that influential adult or upperclassman (see tips #2 and #3), ask them if they know about any clubs that begin meeting or sports that begin practicing before the actual school year begins. If they don't have an answer, find out the name of the person you might call at the high school that would have that information.

It would be a real shame to miss out on an opportunity to get to know fellow students and teachers/coaches. You don't want to have to live with regret as you watch a team play, the drama club perform, the first edition of the school newspaper put out, or the student art show put on, all without you.

In particular, football practice always begins early with double sessions. These are two-a-day practices that usually begin two weeks before the first day of school. At some schools, this includes freshman football, although most often it is just for junior varsity and varsity football. Soccer, field hockey, and volleyball are other fall sports that have double sessions. Be prepared for the intensity of high school sports by getting yourself in shape over the summer, but don't worry too much about not being good enough.

# Relax a little!

## MYTH:

"In high school, this kind of work just WILL NOT DO," says the teacher. "You'd better straighten up and quick!"

### MYTHBUSTER:

*Your middle school teachers will warn you about the rigors of high school. Then your high school teachers will warn you about college. After that, your college professors will warn you about life in "the real world" after you graduate. All of these teachers mean well, but just as you made the adjustment from elementary school to middle school, you'll make the adjustment from middle school to high school.*

# Top Three Reasons to Relax:

1. High school is a time for fun, and you will have fun: dances, bonfires, clubs, sports, friends, parties, fielwd trips, getting your driver's license, movies, the mall without Mom and Dad, earning some money, prom, etc.

2. Those middle school teachers really did get you prepared for high school. All of the work you did for them *will* pay off.

3. Not only will your high school teachers help you to get ready for college or employment, they will help you to be successful in high school. You might be surprised to find that most of them actually enjoy helping you!

# Academics: The first week of school.

# Make a good first impression on your teachers.

As you've heard a million times before, and will hear a million times again, you only have one chance to make a good first impression. Although that first day of school will be one of the most exciting days of your life, don't let your emotions get the best of you. Keep yourself under control and make sure that when your teachers form their opinion of you, it is a positive one.

# "How can I make a good first impression without everyone thinking I'm a dork?"

- Walk, don't run.
- Talk, don't yell.
- **Have all of your materials ready.** A teacher will not be impressed if you ask to borrow a pencil on Day One!
- **Sit in the second row rather than the first row.** You'll be up close without appearing overeager to your classmates. Just don't sit in the back row—that never sends a good message to the teacher.
- **Don't sit next to your friends.** The temptation to talk will be too great.
- **Raise your hand rather than calling out.** This will score points with the teacher and, believe it or not, the other students (who find calling out rude and annoying).
- **If you didn't have the chance to say hello to the teacher when entering the classroom, say goodbye as you're leaving.** Give the teacher reason—a good reason—to remember your face.

# Be organized!

Teacher handouts are numerous, but it is up to you to not lose things like the syllabus and the class grading system.

---

**Syllabus (noun):**

The list of required reading and schedule of assignments, tests, and papers that a teacher gives to each student; if it's more than one page long, you're going to have a lot to do!

---

One last reminder: it isn't enough just to get yourself organized at the beginning of the school year; you have to stay organized throughout the school year. Why not set aside 15 minutes every Sunday to get yourself ready for the week? Remove returned work from your backpack (throw out what you won't need to study for future tests), straighten up your work area, and check your binder reminder, the various syllabi, and your white board or PDA for projects and papers that are due in the upcoming week. And don't be afraid to ask Mom or Dad for help if getting reorganized seems like more than you can handle.

## Organization Checklist:

✓ Set up a "color code" system for each different class so that papers are easy to find
  • Put colored tabs on the divider for each class (red for social studies, blue for English, etc.)
  • Put colored stickers on papers, textbooks (many teachers will ask you to put a book cover on your textbook), and handouts

✓ Use that "binder reminder" assignment pad
  • Any daily assignment pad will do, but the more space you have to write legible notes, the better

✓ At home, arrange your work area like an adult arranges an office at work
  • This might include:
    – An in-box (for work to be completed)
    – An out-box (for completed work)
    – A small whiteboard or chalkboard for reminders
    – A yellow sticky pad for reminders
    – A place to put your computer keyboard (on top of the monitor, under the desk, etc.) so that you have work space for handwritten assignments
    – Supplies including paper clips, tape dispenser, stapler, one-hole or three-hole punch, and any other tools you want to have handy

# Get to know your guidance counselor.

If you've met your new guidance counselor already, stop in to say hi again. If you haven't met your counselor, introduce yourself.

That being said, this is one time that we'll say it's okay to wait a little. Feel free to stop by during the second or third week of school, especially because guidance counselors are always busy changing student schedules during the first week. Besides, you'll have so much going on, it'll probably be hard to remember this tip. But don't let it go for too long. Not only do guidance counselors know how to respond to your needs, they might have answers to questions you haven't even thought of yet!

## Don't Be Afraid to Request a Schedule Change

*You might be one of the students whose schedule needs changing. If, for some reason, your science lab is scheduled at the same time as your lunch, make an appointment with your guidance counselor. Pronto! If you are in a social studies class—global studies, perhaps—with all sophomores and you are a freshman, make an appointment. Pronto! Also, if you took three years of Spanish in middle school, but are now scheduled for French, make that appointment. Ahora!*

# Get to know your teachers— all of them!

You made a good first impression. Now, follow up on it by being respectful and responsible. To state the obvious, don't try to be the class clown. You might impress some of your classmates, but you will not impress your teacher.

By being respectful and attentive, you'll let the teachers get to know the real you, and in turn, they'll be willing to let you know

### "Why do I need to impress my teachers?"

1. You will get better grades.

2. You will have a good reputation.

3. You will experience positive relationships.

more about them. Classes are always more interesting when you understand where your teachers are coming from.

# Get to know your school librarian.

Most teenagers don't get to know the librarians at the public library and the high school library. When you're in a tight spot with a huge research assignment, the librarian can be your best friend.

## Check In with Public Librarians Too

*Use your local library as a resource, as well. Most likely, its collection is bigger than the high school's, and it also has access to the interlibrary loan system. You can get familiar with the library while doing your "summer reading" (tip #5).*

# Top Three Things the Librarian Can Do for You:

1. She is not just a bookworm but also an expert in areas like online research.

2. He can show you how to cite sources properly when writing papers.

3. She will be able to teach you about additional resources—people, books, reading materials, etc.—that you would have no way of knowing about otherwise.

# "If you fail to prepare, be prepared to fail."

As the old saying goes, "If you fail to prepare, be prepared to fail."

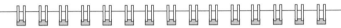

## Top Five Things You're Most Likely to Forget at Home or in Your Locker:

1. **No. 2 pencils**—you're used to bringing pens to class, but you'll need pencils too, especially when taking a standardized test

2. **Highlighters**—they're usually bigger than pens, but you'd be surprised how often students forget to bring them to class

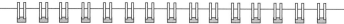

3. **A calculator** for math class (plus whatever other mathematical tools are required)

4. **Lab goggles** for science

5. **A well-rested body and mind,** as well as a positive attitude—you can do it!

# PART THREE

# Academics: Getting your work done and done well.

# Get a good night's sleep and eat a good breakfast.

A well-rested mind and body are important for so many reasons. Nobody needs more sleep than teenagers. It's true. Your body is growing at an incredible rate, and your mind is being taxed by schoolwork. Sleep and eating right allows you to be productive, healthy, and happy!

**Q:** "How much sleep do I really need? And what should I eat for breakfast?"

**A:** **Sleep:** *Somewhere around nine hours a night. Eight hours is the least you should get, although there will be times when you get less. Just realize that it isn't easy to make up for lost sleep.*

**Breakfast:** *You need to chow down heartily, as long as it's a healthy breakfast. Your body needs quality calories just like a car needs gas, so avoid foods whose benefits wear off quickly. You don't want to be hungry again by 9:00, especially if lunch isn't until 12:30! Pop-Tarts have a lot of sugar and you might get a burst of energy, but the natural sugar found in fruit will boost your energy for far longer. Remember that proteins (eggs and bacon) last longer than carbs (bagels) and allow your motor to run on high octane!*

# Don't just work hard, work smart.

When the teacher first assigns that project, don't rest easy knowing the due date is still two weeks off. Get to work right away. But by saying "get to work," we don't mean you should start researching or writing right away. Make a plan for the next two weeks and give yourself a couple of due dates (as opposed to that one due date, imposed on you by the teacher). Take control of your assignment and your schedule.

## "What kinds of due dates should I set for writing a paper?"

- Highlight the important requirements of the paper; decide just how hard it will be and how long it will take you.

- Look at your calendar to see what else you have going on and how much these events and assignments will interfere with completing this paper.

- Make a list and gather up all necessary materials and resources.

- Put together an outline and review it with the teacher or, if your teacher is unavailable, give it to a classmate for feedback.

- Write your rough draft.

- Edit your rough draft and write a second draft.

- Edit your second draft and show it to the teacher or a classmate to get feedback.

- TYPE, don't handwrite, your final draft.

- Most importantly, make sure to have it in your binder on the day that it is due!

# Find a good place to do your homework.

Beware of homework distractions! In your room are most of your favorite things. You might have a TV, a computer with Internet access, or a phone. All of these are evil items dedicated to keeping you from your work!

It might be that your whole house is a little too loud for studying. If so, go to the library or coffee shop after school or maybe a relative's house at night. You might even be able to work somewhere at the school and then take a late bus home.

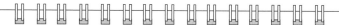

# Put together a mobile office.

- If you're going to use a laptop, make sure the carrying case you have is padded enough to protect it.

- Get a backpack that is big enough for all of your stuff, but don't overload it so as to give yourself back problems. This is seriously an issue for many students.

- Make sure you have a couple of pens and pencils, your binder and binder reminder, the assignments you have to complete (do them in order of importance in case you get distracted), and whatever tools are needed to get the work done.

# Remember to bring home what you need for your homework.

"Of course I'll remember to bring home what I need every day!" you might say. But all too often, students forget things. So, take a moment to double-check your bag before leaving your locker at the end of the day.

The main reason for staying on top of your work is so that you get full credit (most teachers will subtract points for lateness) for your efforts. But another reason is that once you begin to fall behind, the pile of overdue work can seem overwhelming.

## Why Bring It If You Don't Need It?

*If there is a book or something else that you will need to complete a paper or project but won't need in school that day, leave it at home. Your back will appreciate it, and this is the only way to guarantee that you will have it when you sit down to do homework that night.*

# Make lists.

There are "To-Do" lists and "To-Bring" lists and "Don't Forget!" lists too. Any time you can make a visual reminder for yourself, you increase the chances of remembering. Any time you can put that visual reminder where you will see it frequently, you increase those chances even more.

Lists are one example of a helpful visual reminder. The rubber band around the wrist—one for each thing you have to remember to do—is another. When you have a lot to keep track of, though, it's better to have one list rather than 12 rubber bands running up your arm!

## Sample "To-Bring" List:

1. Completed worksheets for social studies

2. Lunch (on a day you want to avoid the cafeteria food!)

3. Rough draft of English paper

4. Biology project proposal

5. Dan's iPod

6. Maria's $2

```
Proposal (noun):

Plan; suggestion; application; an
idea you put down on paper and
present to someone for approval.
```

# Create a nightly schedule.

This is a list that could go on a whiteboard above your desk or on a yellow sticky. It could be numbered, bulleted, or just a checklist. You might even want to note the times next to each item so that you can tell whether or not you're "on schedule."

## MYTH:
Every night you can expect 10 minutes of homework per grade, meaning 90 minutes of homework in 9th grade.

### MYTHBUSTER:
*Some nights you will have a lot of homework (maybe even two hours' worth), and other nights you will have very little homework (party time!).*

## Sample Schedule:

1. Call Alex (5:15)

2. Do Spanish homework (5:30)

3. Eat dinner (6:00)

4. Wash dishes (6:30)

5. Do math and photography homework (6:45)

6. E-mail Cheliq, Kelvin, and Paul (8:00)

7. Watch game (8:45)

8. Write Dana a letter (10:30)

9. Read pages 1–20 in *To Kill a Mockingbird* (11:00)

10. Sleep (11:30) (adjust to give yourself at least eight hours of sleep, depending on when you have to get up—see tip #18)

**NOTE:** *We suggest tackling the most difficult assignment first, when you have the most energy and can give it your all.*

# Keep a calendar in the kitchen.

As the expression goes, you can sometimes "kill two birds with one stone." By making use of a calendar, the two birds are you and your family, the stone is a calendar, and instead of "kill" the verb is "remind." So, remind yourself and your family of upcoming events with a calendar in a central location: the kitchen is probably the best place in the house.

## Remind Yourself and Remind Your Family

**1.** A calendar will remind you of when assignments are due, tests are scheduled, and essays should be written.

**2.** A calendar will remind your family to remind *you* when those assignments are due, tests are scheduled, and essays need to be written.

**3.** A calendar will remind your family to go easy on you in terms of expecting chores to be done and requiring your attendance at family functions when those assignments are due, tests are scheduled, and essays need to be written.

# You can work with study buddies, but be careful.

Our student contributors like the idea of study buddies, just not too often.

It isn't that you should make any sort of "once a week" rule. It's more like you make study buddies a part of your plan to study for a test, but not your *entire* plan. Be sure to do some solo work, as well.

## Pros:

- Your academic weakness may be your buddy's strength.
- Your strength may be your buddy's weakness. Teaching a topic to someone else is good review for you.
- Studying together is fun.
- If you missed something your teacher said, your study buddy hopefully heard it.

## Cons:

- Beware the three Gs: gossiping, giggling, and going out. All three can be fun, but they aren't very productive as far as your schoolwork goes!
- Group work may not be of the same quality as work you complete on your own.
- You might not finish your work.

# Don't always trust the Internet.

The Internet brings a world of information to your very own home, but be wary of the dangers of online encyclopedias when you're doing research. Anyone can contribute information to a Web site like Wikipedia, so double-check before using the "facts" you find there. Any Web site that offers facts but does not cite sources should be avoided. Worst of all are those sites that provide ready-made essays. You should assume that your teacher has seen these before. Besides, the only thing worse than losing points for incorrect info is getting nailed for plagiarism. Students have been expelled from college for turning in work that's not their own.

You might also want to take care when information or advice comes via chat room, instant message, or e-mail. Even well-intentioned people can be wrong, not to mention the folks who will lead you astray on purpose.

## Citing Your Sources

*The American Psychological Association (APA) and
Modern Language Association of America (MLA)
are the two most widely accepted formats for citing
sources (footnotes, endnotes, and bibliography).*

# Recommended
# Online Resources:

- *www.bartelby.com*
- *www.britannica.com*
- *http://encarta.msn.com/Default.aspx*
- *www.infoplease.com/encyclopedia/*
- *www.m-w.com*

# TIP 27

# Budget your time wisely.

Instead of asking, "Why do now what I could do tomorrow?" be **proactive** and proclaim, "Why do tomorrow what I could do now?"

The same way that you need to budget your money, you need to **budget your time.** Both are a limited resource, after all. Besides, it always seems to happen that on the night you are finally ready to dig into a **big project,** another teacher from another class gives you a ton of homework. This is going to happen more than once, and it is a bummer, because it really does throw all of your systems and good planning out the window. The only way you can be prepared is by fighting the urge to put work off.

# Be wise when planning your weekend schedule.

It's Friday night, and the world is yours. No more getting up at the crack of dawn, no more late nights of studying for rumored pop quizzes, no more nagging from Mom and Dad that you can't do something because you've got school tomorrow. Nope, none of that because it's the weekend!

Still, in order to start Monday off right, there will be homework to finish over the weekend. So a plan is in order. Here are two different approaches. Pick the one that works for you; just don't leave everything till Sunday night.

## The Friday Night Plan:

- If nothing special is going on, no good DVDs are lying around, and none of your friends want to hang out, get some (if not all) of your work done.

- The one drawback is you're tired from your week and tired of doing work.

- The one major benefit is if you're able to get a lot of work completed, then you'll have a free and clear weekend.

- One warning: don't try to plow your way through everything just to get it done, especially if you're tired. C is the first letter in careless and a C is what you will get, at best, if you turn in work that you rushed to complete.

## The Spread-It-Out Plan:

- Friday night: before going out or talking on the phone or instant messaging or playing video games or whatever it is you do to relax, complete just one homework assignment. Unlike a regular weeknight, we recommend you do whatever assignment you want, even if it's the easiest one. It is Friday night, after all!

- Saturday: in the morning, after having a breakfast and catching up with your family, complete one more assignment. Then take the rest of the day off.

- Sunday: Whether you do it first thing in the morning or sometime during the afternoon, finish the rest of your homework before dinner. From dinnertime on, you should relax and rest up for your week.

- The one drawback to this plan is that you will have to think about work at least once every day of the weekend.

- The one major benefit to this plan is that you will be able to put your full concentration into each assignment, especially if you have half of the work done before Sunday.

- *One warning:* don't be tempted into leaving everything for Sunday.

# Find out how you will be graded.

**"What percentage of my grade is based on homework, anyway?"**

If a teacher doesn't give you a handout explaining what percentage of your quarterly grade the homework is, be sure to ask. If homework assignments make up 25 percent of the grade and the quarterly exam is also 25 percent of the grade, you know you're going to have to spend a lot of time studying for that test! And if 10 percent of your grade is pop quizzes—or even regularly scheduled quizzes—realize that this is the same as saying that homework counts for 35 percent of your average. Why? Because if you do your homework, you will do well on these quizzes (25% + 10% = 35%). If you aren't "practicing" your work by completing these assignments, you will not do well, and more than a third of your quarterly grade will be unnecessarily low.

## Sample Grading System I:

**25%** Homework

**25%** Research Paper

**25%** Quizzes and Tests

**25%** Class Participation

## Sample Grading System II:

**20%** Homework

**20%** Current Events Summaries

**20%** Quizzes and Tests

**20%** Quarterly Exam

**10%** Class Participation

**10%** Group Presentation

# Improve from quarter to quarter.

As we said earlier, it's important to make a good first impression, but it's also important to maintain that good reputation with your teachers. The worst thing you can do as a student is start out always participating, turning all work in on time, being helpful with other students, being polite and hardworking, and getting good grades—and then when the second quarter comes around, rest on your laurels. Teachers always say the same thing about students who demonstrated, early on, how much they are capable of and then slacked off: "What a waste."

Ninety-nine percent of teachers will tell you that their favorite kind of student is the hard worker. But there is another kind of student who will always leave a good lasting impression:

the student who continually *improves.* For example, the student who struggles a bit during the first quarter and gets a C+, and then improves to a B– the second quarter, followed by a B+ the third quarter, capping the year off by acing the final exam and earning an A for the fourth quarter will always make a teacher smile. So don't despair if you have a shaky start; continued improvement will easily erase a bad first impression.

## Helpful Hint:

*Teachers are optimists. They wouldn't spend their time teaching if they didn't believe that* all *students are capable of learning. Prove them right for having such faith in your capabilities!*

# Make an action plan before progress reports come.

**"If the bad news is going to come, how will it come?"**

Your middle school might not have had progress reports, but chances are your high school does. So be aware of those notices that will arrive five or six weeks into the first quarter.

**"Now that the bad news has come, what can I do?"**

To defuse your angry and/or disappointed parents, and to make sure that the grades go up rather than down, you need to figure out what it will take to improve in each class. You want to see the results immediately (i.e., before the first quarter ends in a couple of weeks), but the most reasonable goal is your second quarter grades. Halfway through freshman year, you don't want to dig such a deep hole that you're still trying to get out of it as a junior or senior.

**"What does an action plan look like?"**

It looks like whatever you want it to look like; more specifically, it should have a design that fits you (on a poster, on a goal contract signed by you and your folks, etc.). Just try to be as specific and realistic as possible.

## Action Plan

**Goal:** Raise algebra average by five points.

**When:** By the end of first quarter.

**How:** Stay after school twice a week and have Mom or Dad quiz me once a week.

# Don't make empty promises.

Hey, everyone stretches the truth every now and again. But be careful of making promises that you might not be able to keep. Not only do you not want to lose people's trust, but failing to deliver also hurts your self-esteem.

**Instead of these promises:**

**1.** "I'll do it tomorrow."

"I promise I won't do that again." **2.**

**3.** "I'm going to change. I swear!"

**Try these:**

**1.** "I promise I'll try to spend more time on homework."

**2.** "I promise I'll ask you for help the next time I don't know something."

**3.** "I'm going to try to improve each of my grades, even if just a little bit, next term."

Not only are the promises in the second group *specific* ("more time," "ask you for help," and "improve each of my grades"), they are *realistic*. The person who promises to turn a D into an A by next quarter is setting everyone up for a disappointment.

# Stay after school for extra help.

Your middle school teachers probably didn't offer after-school help, but high school teachers will usually offer after-school help one or two days a week. Take advantage.

It is also wise not only to self-monitor but to self-initiate when it comes to getting help and raising your grades. Here's the plan:

```
Self-initiate (verb):

To get yourself started; to make the
first move; to take control and get your
rear in gear!
```

**1.** Recognize when things are not going well. Pay attention when work is handed back and face up to low grades and test scores.

**2.** Ask for an appointment with your teacher. Don't keep waiting for the invitation that might never come; many teachers will only help those who help themselves.

**3.** Before or after the review session starts, ask your teacher what you can do to boost your average: Study differently? Hand in extra credit work? Stay after school once or twice a week, every week?

```
Self-monitor (verb):

To check or supervise yourself; to keep
an eye on yourself so other people,
mainly your parents, don't have to.
```

# Take advantage of "office hours" too.

After-school help is the opportunity to work with the teacher in a small group setting; making an appointment during office hours means the opportunity to have a one-on-one question-and-answer session with your teacher.

## Don't Waste Anyone's Time:

*Many doctors complain that their patients will often "hide" what's really ailing them, talking about everything but the real problem. Don't do this with your teacher when discussing your struggles! Their time is limited, as is yours, so after a minute of small talk, get to the point. Ask some good, well-thought out questions.*

## What to Ask About

✓ That lesson you didn't really understand

✓ The one homework problem you were unable to complete

✓ Upcoming projects and tests

✓ How you're doing this quarter

✓ If there's any extra credit you can do

# Prioritize when there are scheduling conflicts.

Scheduling conflicts with after-school help and office hours are bound to happen when you're taking six or seven different classes, so don't be surprised when you have to choose between after-school help *or* office hours for different classes. This is really a decision of now or later, one teacher getting your attention and attendance now while the other gets it later.

# Prioritization Planner:

1. Go where the next big test or project is due (no translation needed!).

2. Go where the concepts currently being covered are the most difficult (translation: think about the class that is confusing you the most *right now*).

3. Go where you have the lowest grade average (translation: the effort to raise your grades includes putting in extra time and extra work).

4. Go where you have not gone in a long time (translation: if you've been neglecting a certain class, make that teacher's office hours or extra help session a priority).

# Ask about extra credit.

A wise person once said that you should never ask someone to help you solve a problem unless you already have a solution in mind.

The point is, when you go to ask a teacher for some extra-credit work, it will be worth your while to have one or two assignments in mind. If not, you run the risk of hearing no or, even worse, being handed busywork. Busywork serves very little purpose and will hardly be worth the extra credit you receive. Why? Because when you do extra-credit work it should be more than just a gesture; it should be a way for you to pull your grade up while also gaining additional understanding of the curriculum.

## Extra-Credit Ideas Checklist:

✓ Find a current events article relating to concepts currently being studied and write a summary.

✓ Write a summary of an important chapter from the textbook.

✓ Write definitions and/or sentences for important vocabulary words.

✓ Create an extra-credit quiz (with answer key) that the teacher might offer to other students who are looking for some extra work.

✓ While you are brainstorming extra-credit ideas for your teacher, don't forget to look into rewriting papers or retaking tests. Some teachers will turn you down, but many others will say yes. And you won't know until you ask, so ask!

```
Curriculum (noun):

The material to be covered, and tested,
during the year in a certain class.
```

# Get on the honor roll and earn some respect.

Earning Mom and Dad's trust has many benefits. So does earning their respect. If the question is about how you can earn it, then the answer, for once, is simple: get on the honor roll. Better yet, get high honors.

What the honor roll and high honors consist of is pretty consistent across different high schools. Essentially, think about getting As. You get As and you get honor roll. You get honor roll, you get respect.

### "But what do I have to do to earn honor roll?"

**Honor Roll Requirements:** *An overall grade point average of 90 percent or higher in all classes.*

**High Honor Roll Requirements:** *An overall grade point average of 95 percent or higher in all classes.*

**Other:** *Some schools will also recognize students with an overall grade point average that falls between 85 percent and 90 percent. Rather than honor roll, it's more like an honorable mention.*

## Grade Translation

| | | | | |
|---|---|---|---|---|
| A+ | = | 98% | = | 3.8 |
| A | = | 95% | = | 3.5 |
| A– | = | 92% | = | 3.2 |
| B+ | = | 88% | = | 2.8 |
| B | = | 85% | = | 2.5 |
| B– | = | 82% | = | 2.2 |
| C+ | = | 78% | = | 2.8 |
| C | = | 75% | = | 2.5 |
| C– | = | 72% | = | 2.2 |

NOTE: There's no need to describe grades that are lower than this as you will not be earning grades any lower than this. Right?

# Create your own incentive plan.

Now that you're in high school, you've got to figure out how to motivate yourself. Why? Because if you don't experiment and find a way now, you will struggle in college and in your job. Work it out now, and the exact opposite will happen: you'll experience success wherever you go.

So set yourself some personal goals and do all you can to reach them. These goals should not just be thoughts in your head, either. Write them down and read them often. You can even change your goals throughout the year (or over the years).

```
Incentive (noun):

Motivation in the form of a prize or
reward; something you want!
```

## "How should I remind myself of my goals?"

**1.** Put the goals on a poster board and post it on your bedroom wall.

**2.** E-mail the list of goals to your best friend and ask your friend to e-mail them back to you once a week.

**3.** Have your parents ask you for updates, which include not just accomplished goals but what you have done to work toward accomplishing the remaining goals.

## "What's the incentive?"

**1.** Experiencing success in school

**2.** All that respect from Mom and Dad

**3.** And finally, the subject of this section: rewarding yourself for success. For each goal that you write down, you should also note what you will give yourself or do for yourself once that goal is reached: a new DVD, downloading 50 songs, new clothes, or whatever you like!

# Seek out incentive plans.

Often, local businesses will offer incentive plans of their own as a form of advertising. Teenagers are actually an attractive customer group for businesses—including online retailers—because teenagers tend to have disposable income, so look there for incentive plans, as well.

So ask around town. Does the music store give a discount for an A? Free fries from the fast-food joint for Bs or higher?

Two tickets to the movies? Dessert at the coffee shop? If they don't have one already, you might suggest an incentive plan to store owners, or have a friend who works there make the suggestion.

Usually it works like this: you walk into the store with a copy of your report card and some form of ID and then walk out with some cool merchandise. Not a bad deal, huh?

```
Disposable income (noun):

Money not required for "needs," like
rent, the electric bill, or gas; money
that can be spent on "wants," such as
concert tickets, MP3 players, etc.
```

# How to deal with extenuating circumstances.

So far, these tips have been given under the assumption that you are of a clear mind, in top-notch health, and wake up every morning fully capable of giving 100 percent at school. That isn't always going to be the case, though. Of course, you've been sick before, but now that you're in high school, you are expected to be more responsible for yourself. Even when faced with extenuating circumstances—like sickness, an appointment, or a death in the family—there are ways to handle yourself that will help keep you from falling behind.

---

**Extenuating circumstances (noun):**

Situations that are out of the ordinary but do have an explanation.

## Top Five Ways to Deal with Extenuating Circumstances:

1. *Keep up your attendance when you're feeling well so that your absences aren't too damaging when you're truly sick.*

2. *It's better to show up at school and leave a little early than not to show up at all. Missing just one or two classes is better than missing all six or seven.*

3. *Make sure you don't end up spending more time in the nurse's office than in class.*

4. *To the best of your ability, you should try to miss no more than two or three days per quarter and no more than ten days over the course of the year. In some districts, 20 absences (with or without a doctor's notes) means a trip to court for you and your parents.*

5. *Have a friend or sibling get your assignments for you when you're out; otherwise, you'll be swamped with work when you return.*

```
Repercussion (noun):

An effect or outcome; can be really
good or really bad.
```

# What you should do during a sick day.

Too many teenagers get too little sleep. So on your day off, be sure to get plenty of rest. Whether it's in bed or on the couch, be immobile. Get horizontal. Relax!

Now the bad news. While relaxing, take a break from the remote control and phone (all your friends are in class, anyway) and pick up a book. Even if it isn't reading for school, give your mind a little exercise. Even if it's just a chapter or two.

Finally, remember to have someone bring your homework home for you. Call the office at the school and give the name of a friend to one of the secretaries. By day's end, your friend should be able to gather a couple of assignments for you, and after a day of rest, you'll be ready to sit up and do some work.

## Sick Day Checklist:

✓ Vitamin C

✓ A little bit of rest and a little bit of reading

✓ A call to school for your homework

✓ A little more rest!

# What to do after returning from a sick day.

Now that you're feeling better, it's time to play catch-up. Even if you got all of your homework assignments from a friend and completed each and every one of them, you missed important information when you missed each teacher's lesson. When an adult returns to work, there is a to-do pile on the desk and a ton of phone messages and e-mails that need to be returned. For you, it's the previous day's curriculum (from all six or seven classes) that requires your immediate attention.

## MYTH:

Your friends will be able to fill you in on all that you missed.

### MYTHBUSTER:

*Only your teachers can truly fill you in. Arrive two minutes early to class or stay two minutes late and ask about what you missed and what you can do to catch up.*

# What to do, and not do, when your teacher is absent.

**What Not to Do:** Don't listen to the kids who say, "After ten minutes we're free to go. Just put your name on the board for attendance." They are basing this on urban myth and definitely not on school policy! If you leave, the teacher will be angry because you are that teacher's responsibility. In turn, if the teacher is absent and 15 minutes into the class an assistant principal shows up to find nobody there, you know there's going to be **trouble.** Schools really don't want a whole class full of students wandering the halls!

**To Do:** Sit and wait. Talk. Use the class as a study hall. This is probably the **best bet of all,** considering everybody else in the room is expected to learn all of the same material you are. Whatever you do, just **don't leave the room** until a staff member tells you to do so.

# What you should do the day before and the day after a school vacation.

The school may be half-empty, as the lucky and the lazy are absent, but rather than joining the crowd, seize the opportunity to spend time getting extra help from a teacher. Let the teacher get to know you in a calmer, quieter environment. You might not be one of the lucky ones going on vacation, but you could find that your luck has come in the form of an extra point or two on your quarterly grade. Teachers are humans too, and they're liable to give a little boost to a student they know and like.

## MYTH:

If your average for the quarter works out to an 89.75 percent, the teacher will laugh wickedly and round you down to an 89 percent.

### MYTHBUSTER I:

*If your average for the quarter works out to an 89.75 percent and the teacher is an objective grader, you will, by the rules of math, be rounded up to a 90 percent.*

### MYTHBUSTER II:

*If your average for the quarter works out to an 89.75 percent and the teacher thinks highly of you, the teacher might end up giving you a boost up to a 91 percent or 92 percent. How nice!*

# Find out how to get around school when injured.

In middle school, the students probably weren't trusted with the keys to the elevator, but in high school, the administrators will, more times than not, empower their injured students to get around the building as quickly and as safely as possible. So be proactive when you've broken an arm or blown out a knee. Asking a few questions and making a few requests could make your life a lot easier during this frustrating time.

Stop by the front office with your doctor's note and ask what you can do to make sure you can get to class on time. Is there an elevator you can take up to your science class? Is there a parking spot for the temporarily handicapped? Can you be first in line for lunch and grab a seat in the cafeteria before the mad rush begins?

Perhaps most important of all is the note you get not from your doctor but from the principal. This is the note that reads something like this: "Please allow (your name) to arrive in class up to three minutes late and to leave class three minutes early."

Life just got a little better! The hallways are crazy in between classes, and a permission slip like this is sure to help. And it's sad but true: if you don't ask the teachers or principal, they might never think to offer.

# Figure out who you are and what matters to you.

Freshman year is important for you as a student. You will form study habits to carry you through all four years of high school, and you will find out what you might want to study in college. But freshman year—high school, in general—is also important in a more personal way. As you grow from a 13-year-old to an 18-year-old, you will make the transition from childhood to adulthood. You will form friendships that might last a lifetime. You will make decisions about the kind of person you want to be and the kind of person, or people, you want to be with. Wow!

The same way that you'll want to keep your eyes and ears open for everything going on around you, you'll want to make decisions using both your heart and your head. When something bad happens, you'll want to make sure that you don't get too down about it, and when something great happens, you'll want to enjoy the moment but not get too out of control with the celebrating. Keeping your emotions in balance is a skill that will benefit you throughout your life.

If something happens to make you unhappy or uncomfortable, that's when the toughest decisions need to be made. You might even have to end a friendship with someone who's acting in a hurtful or self-destructive way. But if you are careful with such decisions, asking others for advice and always staying true to yourself, by the time you graduate, you'll really know who you are.

# Sit, listen, and learn.

## MYTH:
School assemblies are corny. They're stupid.
A total waste of time. Boo!

### MYTHBUSTER:
*School assemblies are rarely as corny as they
seem. These days, with all of the standardized
tests, schools can't afford to waste time with
pointless presentations. If a speaker is brought
in, the message* must *be important.*

So while you're sitting there, try to listen. You
might learn something unexpected. And for the
first time in this book, we will give the advice
that you NOT do your homework while you're
sitting there. Resist the urge to talk, to text
message, to sleep. Sit, listen, and learn.

## Top Three School Assemblies:

1. **Personal Health:** eating habits, the dangers of drugs and alcohol, mental health, family planning, etc.

2. **Safety in School:** discussing crisis plans is the most common.

3. **Fundraising:** companies will make presentations to clubs, your class, or the entire school.

## Buddy/Mentor/Peer-to-Peer Programs

*These school-organized activities are also a good use of your time. As a freshman, you'll be assigned an older student that will work with you on academics and answer any personal questions you have. Experiences like this are far from corny and were often cited by contributors to this book as one of the most worthwhile experiences in high school. So sit, listen, and learn when a teacher, guidance counselor, or administrator is telling you about such programs. You won't regret it.*

# PART FOUR

# Extracurricular activities.

# Get connected!

There's no better feeling than having good friends around; people you can trust and whose company you enjoy! This network includes family members and other adults in your life. When there are things going on that your family might not understand, and your friends might not have the perspective you need, it would be great to have an adult at school to turn to. And when you're feeling down about things, don't keep your feelings in, because the stress will only build up. Too many other teens have had a hard time, and some of them dropped out of school or worse. Rather than become a statistic, establish those connections so that you'll have a support system at school.

## "Who should I 'get connected' with?"

- Friends who have common interests and take similar classes
- Coaches and club advisors
- Favorite teacher
- Guidance counselor
- Trusted administrator

## "How do I 'get connected'?"

- Join clubs and/or teams. Not only will you meet other students, you will get to know the advisor.
- When you meet someone with similar interests, make the effort to become friends.
- Have conversations with other students or adults, even if it's just small talk. Tip #2 recommends forming a relationship with your teachers and guidance counselor early on, and this is one reason why.
- Be there for others, and they will be there for you.

# Busy people tend to stay busy.

## MYTH:

If I don't play a sport, join a club, and get a job, then I will do really, really well in school.

### MYTHBUSTER I:

*If you always a have a ton of free time, it's very, very difficult to buckle down and get all of your work done during the busy times.*

### MYTHBUSTER II:

*Those who have to figure out how to balance their schedules have an easier time planning what to do (and when to do it!) during the busy times.*

As an adult, you'll get a credit card and then, a couple of years later, a mortgage to buy a house. Having that credit card will actually help you get a mortgage. This is because companies that give loans are impressed by people who've borrowed money and paid it back. They're much more willing to loan money to the person who has proven they're responsible. By proving you can balance your schedule on a day-to-day basis, you'll actually improve your ability to handle everything during extremely busy times.

The student who's always on the go, handling academic, social, and extracurricular activities, has practice in dealing with extreme time demands. When midterms and finals come around, this student stands a better chance of being successful with schoolwork. It's true!

# Playing sports is a matter of balance!

If you play a sport, you'll have practice every afternoon, and this means not getting home until just before dinnertime. On game nights, you'll get home even later, so discipline is needed. After all, your teachers still expect your homework to be completed.

The best thing you can do is establish a nighttime routine for practice nights (homework, then dinner, then homework) and one for game nights (dinner then homework, get to bed early, and then wake up early to finish your homework). Notice how in both sample schedules, there is no socializing. No phone calls. No TV. No Internet. The easiest way to compensate for your sports schedule is by cutting out those "free time" activities. Keep this in mind when deciding whether or not to play a sport, but also realize there are academic benefits to joining a team. For example, chances are a couple of your teammates will be in your classes, so why not look for a "study buddy" for the bus ride home after a game? Leave the pens and paper in your bag—this is just an opportunity for the two of you to verbally review what's going on in class. Also, your coach might be a teacher and a useful resource. As mentioned in tip #48, establishing connections has a lot of benefits; having teammates and coaches to talk to about schoolwork is one of them.

```
Compensate (verb):
To balance out or make up for.
```

# Ask about getting physical education credit.

While discussing sports, it's worth noting that you won't necessarily have to take gym class if you regularly participate in a sport outside of school.

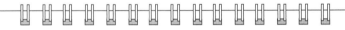

## Top Five Individual, Nonscholastic Sports

1. Swimming
2. Figure skating
3. Equestrian sport
4. Martial arts
5. Fencing

**Exemption (noun):**

Permission to be released from a responsibility.

Here's how it usually works. If you practice more than four or five hours a week, outside of school, then you're probably eligible for an exemption from physical education. Ask your guidance counselor or the athletic director; maybe even have Mom or Dad make the phone call. It will be worth it, academically, as you can now plug a study hall into your schedule. And isn't that important, considering you're using a couple of hours of free time, every day, to play a sport?

# Look into *all* of the clubs.

Athletes play high school sports hoping against hope that someday they might be able to play professional sports, or at least big-time college sports. But did you know, the same kinds of thoughts apply to those who join clubs?

Not only can clubs be a place for exploring professional possibilities; there's a far greater chance of your becoming a Spanish interpreter, a business leader, or a professional photographer than earning a spot in the NBA! The idea is to match your interests today with your interests for the future and see what your school has to offer. At least try to put your time into a club that will help you to get into the college of your choice.

## Potential Clubs:

- Animation/art/photography
- Chess
- Community service
- Debate team
- Drama club
- Drill team
- Family, Careers, and Community Leaders of America (FCCLA)
- Foreign languages
- Forensics
- Future Business Leaders of America (FBLA)
- Key Club
- International Thespian Society
- Yearbook/newspaper/magazine
- Math team
- National Honor Society
- Political
- Students Against Drunk Driving (SADD) or Mothers Against Drunk Driving (MADD)
- School spirit
- Science

Note: Some clubs might meet during lunch, which may or may not be better for you, depending on your after-school schedule.

# Start your own club.

It's worth noting that at some point there were no clubs. There were just classes! But then, a student had an interest. Perhaps it was computers or maybe a school magazine for fiction writers. Whatever it was, that student found a willing teacher and asked the teacher to run the club. As time went by, more and more students asked more and more teachers to be advisors, and more and more clubs emerged. If there's something missing at your school— skateboarding, orienteering, calligraphy—start asking around. See if there's an interest among the students, and then put to use your best sales skills and convince some willing adult to support you.

# Start-a-Club Checklist:

✓ List of interested students

✓ Advisor (an adult, but not necessarily a teacher)

✓ Funding

Chances are, your club will need some supplies, and you can't buy supplies without funding! During the first year, your funds might have to come from a private source. Talk to businesses in town; have members talk to their parents.

✓ A room to meet in and day, or days, of the week when everyone can meet

✓ Publicity to get support from the administration and to recruit more members

# Take part in student government.

When you're on the inside (on the student council, for example), you get a better understanding of how your school works and how decisions are made. You see why the bonfire at homecoming was cancelled and why the prom is being held in the gym rather than at a country club. You see what you can do to make sure those things don't happen during *your* senior year. You'll gain access to the school's administrators, and this is a very good thing when trying to make your high school experience as great as possible. Having been the class president or a class representative will look good when you apply to college too. It shows that you're motivated and like to be involved.

```
Credentials (noun):

Qualifications.
```

## How to Run for Student Government:

1. *Ask somebody to be your campaign manager (input from others is important).*

2. *Collect the required number of signatures so that you can be on the ballot.*

3. *Put up signs that advertise your credentials.*

4. *Find a creative way to put your name in the minds of your classmates (buttons, pencils, T-shirt giveaway, something on a Web site like myspace.com).*

5. *Write a speech and have others edit it for you.*

6. *Practice your speech and then deliver it with confidence and eye contact when the time comes—get all of those students excited!*

Once you win, be sure to work hard to represent the students who elected you. Attend all of the meetings and, just like with sports and clubs, make sure to keep up with your schoolwork. You have to be a student first.

And if you don't win, you can still contribute. Student councils are always looking for volunteers. There are decisions to be made and funds to be raised. Get involved!

# Participate in extracurricular activities outside of school.

Tip #51 made mention of participating in sports outside of high school. There are also other kinds of activities that take place away from the campus that can benefit you as a person and student.

One example is the Boys and Girl Scouts of America. There's Varsity Scouting and Eagle Scouts for boys, Studio 2B for girls, and even a co-ed program called Venturing. Respected as both a leadership and community service activity, this is exactly the kind of experience that's appealing to college admissions officers. Similarly, most houses of worship will offer their younger members opportunities for extracurricular activities. Learning more about your faith means learning more about yourself, and that's always a good thing!

> **Extracurricular (adjective):**
> Additional or optional.

Some towns offer programs through their recreation department. Although people usually associate "recreation" with sports, this isn't always the case. Just as you can find arts programs at Boy's and Girl's Clubs, the same can be said of recreation offices. Check out the bulletin boards at the library or outside of the guidance offices at the high school. The local newspaper is another good source of information, as are the adults in your family or—surprise, surprise!—the adults you've made a connection with at school.

# Find others that share your passion.

It only makes sense that there be talk of preparing for college in a book that's supposed to prepare you for high school. Making your way through school is a progression, and of course you're going to have an eye on the future as you go from 9th grade to 12th grade. But part of a happy existence is finding and pursuing your passions and finding others who share the same interests.

Whenever you join a large team or a popular club, you'll find a variety of interests, personality types, and levels of seriousness in terms of attitude toward the activity. In smaller clubs, though, you stand a chance of finding far greater seriousness and dedication. A greater portion of the conversations will be focused on the activity itself, and the distractions will be far fewer. If it's chess, for example, and there are only five people in the club, the students involved will receive more attention and instruction from the advisor than a baseball player will on a team with 20 other players. Also, some of those athletes might just be playing to do something with their friends. But if there are only five students involved in the chess club, they are obviously dedicated to learning all they can about the game.

So don't avoid a club just because it seems unpopular. Join up and reap the rewards. You'll be happy you did.

```
Passion (noun):

Enthusiasm.
```

# Think local, act local.

Even if community service isn't a passion of yours, it'd be a real shame to go through high school without giving a little something back. Just as it's wise to find your passion, it's a good idea to "act local" (translation: contribute to your hometown).

A lot of kids go through their four years of high school just trying to have as much fun as possible, but it's far better to get into the newspaper for being a Citizen of the Week than it is to end up in the police blotter. And looking toward the future, plenty of people go off to college, then come back to live in their hometown. If this is the case for you, wouldn't you rather have people remember your good deeds and welcome you back with open arms?

**Q:** "How can I help?"

**A:** *There's no shortage of community service opportunities. The Big Brothers Big Sisters program is one example of older kids helping younger kids: everything from taking them out for ice cream to sitting with them while they do their homework. There are also beautification projects to help towns keep clean. There are soup kitchens in cities both big and small, and there are even programs to train teens to be paramedics, firefighters, and police officers. This might be too much for you, but the point is this: there are plenty of ways that you can help.*

# Find a good fit when community service is *required*.

Some schools require their students to perform community service, and although this is rare, it just might be the case for you. Rather than thinking of it as a "requirement," why not think of it as an opportunity?

Community service shouldn't just be an "opportunity" to spend more time with your friends, though. Tip #56 focused on finding your passion, and community service is yet another opportunity to do some searching. Explore an interest and find out if a certain activity is actually a passion of yours. You won't enjoy pulling weeds if gardening isn't of interest to you, so don't do it just because your friend is. And if you don't like books and aren't too sure about spending time with little kids, why volunteer for a reading program? Do what you want to do or, at least, what you think you might want to do. There are a lot of activities in which "you only get out of it what you put into it." Community service is one of them.

And realize that if your school has made community service a requirement, it's for good reason: the faculty cares about your growth as a person just as much as they care about your education.

## Community Service Projects and Organizations:

- Environmental protection/maintenance
- League of Women Voters
- Rotary Club
- Youth Service America
- The Red Cross
- Police Benevolent Association
- Senior citizens' centers
- Handicapped services (The Special Olympics is one very popular organization/event)
- Alcohol, tobacco, and drug awareness
- Neighborhood safety
- Neighborhood beautification
- Promoting literacy

# How will your class give back?

There's giving in the community service sense, and then there's giving as in gifts. Just as you want to be remembered as a good citizen, your class should be motivated to leave a legacy at the high school. This legacy should include the general attitude and behavior of the class as well as the class gift to be given to the principal at graduation. And graduation will come sooner than you can believe.

Hopefully you will have a role in your class' student government. In the least, you can serve on the class gift committee. If so, the goal is to make sure that in the years building up to spring of your senior year, funds are being raised and the students in your class are being polled to find out what they'd like to donate to the school.

## Top Five Class Gift Ideas:

1. A roadside sign with the school's name on it

2. Benches for sitting in a common area or outside where the busses drop off and pick up

3. A bookshelf in the library, stocked with new reference books like encyclopedias or atlases

4. A tree to be planted in a prominent location

5. A clock or sign to greet students as they enter the high school each morning

```
Prominent (adjective):
```
Important or well known.

# Explore your spiritual options.

During high school, there are many distractions and, of course, many of them are fun. You might go through a phase where those distractions seem more important to you than your family. Have your fun, but don't lose perspective on what's really important.

In many families, attending religious worship is a priority, and there's no reason for you to skip out on a tradition like Sunday morning mass just so that you can sleep in. Go with your family, and then come home and take a nap. You might even want to be a little proactive.

If you're feeling curious, ask if you can attend services with a friend. Whether at a church or synagogue or mosque, this is an opportunity to learn about a different culture and religion. You aren't turning your back on your family or religion, and you aren't losing sight of your priorities. You're merely learning more about the world around you.

If you're considering exploring other spiritual options but are feeling a bit guilty about it, ask your parents if it's okay with them. You can even consult with a religious leader. Chances are, you'll receive supportive advice. If you weren't raised in a spiritual home but want to see what the world has to offer, this tip applies to you too! Religious studies is actually a major in college. Why not start learning now?

# PART FIVE

# After-school jobs.

# TIP 61

# Learn about labor laws.

Let's get this first piece of advice out of the way, right away: you might want to wait until your sophomore year to get a job. There's already so much going on as you adjust to high school that having to log hours at work will make it even harder to do well in school, keep up with your social life, and actually see your family. That being said, when the time comes (usually at the age of 14), you'll be able to get your "working papers," or employment certificate, at school. These are the documents that potential employers will ask for when you apply. Make sure you have them and then start checking the want ads. Keep in mind that your age will dictate what you are able to do. For example, you cannot use certain kinds of machinery until you are a certain age, so don't apply for the warehouse job that requires operating a forklift! There are also labor laws relating to how many hours you can work per week, so keep that in mind when applying.

There's another benefit to waiting until you are a sophomore: you will actually be old enough to work a decent number of hours.

## "Is there anything else I'll have to submit with my working papers?"

 Parent/guardian signature

Your birth certificate or baptismal record for proof of age

 A doctor's note stating you're physically fit to work

### From the U.S. Department of Labor Web site (*www.dol.gov*):

*The Fair Labor Standards Act (FLSA) sets wage, hours worked, and safety requirements for minors (individuals under age 18) working in jobs covered by the statute... As a general rule, the FLSA sets 14 years of age as the minimum age for employment, and limits the number of hours worked by minors under the age of 16... However, at any age, youth may deliver newspapers; perform in radio, television, movie, or theatrical productions; work in businesses owned by their parents (except in mining, manufacturing, or hazardous jobs); and perform babysitting or perform minor chores around a private home.*

# Settle for a summer job.

**"A summer job sounds good, but what do I do for spending money during the year?"**

OK, so money is a necessity. It's awfully hard to have fun without it, right? Well, there is a compromise, and it's called summer vacation. You could get a job and earn some cash without impacting your studies.

The catch is this: you'll have to make sure you don't spend it all over the summer. With concerts and movies and road trips and amusement parks and baseball games and everything else, it'll be awfully tempting to spend everything you earn. Great discipline is required. Having a savings account will help.

So in April, hit the bank to open that account and start searching the want ads in your local newspaper. Jobs will be posted there as well as on bulletin boards at the town hall, in the library, or at school outside of the guidance office. There might even be some online job sites for youths in your area.

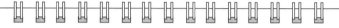

## Top Five Summer Jobs:

1. Summer camp counselor
2. Babysitter
3. Ice cream scooper
4. Municipal worker
   This could be an office job (making copies, running errands, and answering phones) or a maintenance-type job that can include everything from cutting grass to painting fire hydrants and parking meters
5. Retail store clerk

# Find a flexible schedule.

If you have to work during the school year, as many people do, try to find a job that allows you to have a flexible schedule. Waiting tables at a restaurant isn't a great job for a student, unless the restaurant has a young staff and everybody needs to switch hours every once in a while. The best bet is taking a job babysitting or cutting grass. Jobs like these allow some leeway in terms of saying no or asking if you can do the work on a different day.

No matter what kind of job you have, always let the boss know well in advance when you're going to have a scheduling conflict. Try to find somebody to switch with first—so you can tell your boss the work is covered, thus minimizing headaches!—but don't go ahead and schedule the switch, assuming that the boss won't mind.

Flexibility is key not just in high school, but also in life. And it cuts both ways, meaning you should keep in mind that in order to find flexibility, you must also be flexible yourself. Switch with somebody at work when they ask you to.

# Map out the pros and cons.

Research shows that it's easier for people to understand difficult concepts if they're presented in words and in some sort of picture form. This is why teachers will have you use graphic organizers and other such visual aids.

The same can be said when you're problem solving. And it is indeed "problem solving" when you're trying to arrange a schedule that will keep everybody happy while also helping you to be successful in all that you do. When dealing with decisions about how to prioritize what you'll do and when, get yourself a big piece of paper and draw a line right down the middle. On the left side, write "Pros" for the positives. On the right side, write "Cons" for the negatives. Then, start brainstorming. You might even want to ask somebody to help you, especially somebody who has proven that they're good at balancing all of the things in their life.

## Deciding Whether to Work at the Video Store

**Pros:** $6 an hour, only three days a week for a total of 12 hours, one free movie rental per week.

**Cons:** Inflexible schedule, have to work one weekend night, must buy two company shirts ($21 each) as part of the uniform.

# Consider transportation issues.

Like getting to school before the first bell every day, you'll be expected to arrive at work on time. If you're working three nights a week, that means three times a week that you'll be expected at your place of employment—on time! This also means that three times a week, you'll want to get home as soon as possible once work is done. How will you get there? How will you get home? Will getting you back and forth be such a hassle that eventually your ride bails?

## Modes of Transportation:

- Mom, Dad, or older sibling
- Bike, rollerblade, skateboard, scooter, or moped
- City bus
- Walk

If you have to get a ride from somebody, this could present a problem. So if possible, get a job close enough to home that you can get yourself back and forth. For many people, this isn't possible. But just keep it in mind. You might have a choice between two jobs and end up taking the less attractive of the two because it's closer to home.

# Managing your money.

Tip #62 made mention of one of the keys to success for people just entering the working world: opening a savings account. Although the interest you'll earn on your money won't turn you into Donald Trump overnight, your *ability* to save money rather than spend it will increase, because the cash will be in that account rather than crying out "Spend me!" from your wallet.

You might even want to open *two* savings accounts. One could be for your spending money now, while the other is for someday down the road. The rule with this second account is simple: never, ever touch it. Pretend it isn't there. If you get $100 for your birthday, put $50 into one account and $50 into the other. Let money in that "no touch" account accumulate, and maybe someday you can go on vacation with friends or get a new car. You could even save for college!

## "What do I need to save for?"

**Answer #1** *is obvious: save money so you can do really, really fun stuff with your friends. For example, if there are three nights that your friends decide to go to the movies and you stay home to study or rent a movie instead, you save your money so you'll be able to afford to go with them to that concert later. And what sounds better, the movies or a concert?*

**Answer #2** *isn't so obvious but is twice as attractive: within a few years, you'll be old enough to get your driver's license. Wouldn't it be nice to be able to buy yourself a used car? And keep in mind, insurance is expensive for teen drivers. Manage your money, and maybe you'll be able to afford both.*

# Gain experience in an internship.

Admittedly, internships don't pay, but if you find the right one, then the experience you'll gain will go way beyond any dollar value.

Everybody knows it's hard to put long-term benefits ahead of short-term benefits. Most freshmen would have a difficult time choosing something that will look good on the college application or lead to a career over something that can be enjoyed now. Most freshmen would say, "Forget the internship. I'll take the job that pays $6 an hour!" Don't be most freshmen. Be the freshman that fully understands how long-term benefits pay off in far greater numbers (those numbers might be dollars or the number of colleges that accept you) than the short-term benefits.

**Q:** "OK, but what kinds of places offer internships?"

**A:** *Often, offices like to have an intern or two around. (Office work is considered "white-collar.") It might be a doctor's office or an architect's office. It could be a sports marketing firm or an advertising agency. Blue-collar internship opportunities (hands-on work) might also exist. You could learn about plumbing or masonry, for example. Whatever it is, try to match your interests with a company, or individual employer, that will be willing to show you the ropes.*

## Internship (noun):

A job that offers no pay or, at best, a stipend to cover expenses like the commute and lunch.

# Whatever you decide, remember "class before cash!"

Extracurricular activities can really make or break your high school experience. The work you do and the money you earn, the fun you have playing a sport or joining a club, the volunteering you do or the experience you gain in an internship—all could end up being as influential in your life as any class you take or teacher you talk to. Just keep in mind that you're in school to learn. Make your class responsibilities the priority and never take your eyes off of your ultimate goal. Whether it's college, a job, the military, travel, or something else, work hard to make that dream come true. Dabble in some other activities, earn a couple of extra bucks, but keep academics at the forefront of your mind. It's your academic performance that will ultimately decide where you go next, even if it isn't college.

## Put It in Your Memory

*Just remember: "Class before cash! Class before cash!! Class before cash!!!" Having a reminder like this will help you to stay on the right path.*

# PART SIX

# Social life.

# Finding the balance with friends.

Just as was discussed in tip #67, you've got to think about long-term benefits even when it comes to friends. Actually, this is true in all kinds of social situations.

Of course, you always want to treasure your friendships, but keep in mind that friendships aren't always good for you. In fact, sometimes they can be the least healthy, least productive part of your life. If a friend is getting in the way of your reaching your full potential, you've got to ask yourself if their friendship is really worth it. If this friendship has short-term benefits but will hurt you in the long term, should you make a change? Probably. You can break up with a boyfriend or a girlfriend if the relationship is not working, so why not "break up" with a friend if he isn't treating you right or if she is doing things (e.g., illegal or immoral stuff) you don't like?

Fortunately, most of the time less drastic action is necessary. It might be hanging out one or two fewer nights per week with a friend who isn't as serious about schoolwork, and the future, as you are. Or it might be that you really like hanging out with an older friend but refuse to be in the car together, because you've seen how unsafe that person can be behind the wheel. The point is to make sure that you don't damage yourself—physically, emotionally, or academically—because of a friendship.

People change, so don't be surprised if your group of friends changes at least once during your high school years. It might even happen during freshman year as you move out of that middle school mind-set. Whatever happens, be sure to call your own shots. With friends, it doesn't have to be all or nothing; it's a matter of finding a healthy balance.

# Finding the balance with your boyfriend/ girlfriend.

**MYTH:**
If I have a girlfriend or boyfriend, I have to make that person the number-one priority in my life.

MYTHBUSTER:
*Having a boyfriend or girlfriend is a normal part of life and needs to fit into your life in a healthy, productive way.*

Having a boyfriend or girlfriend doesn't mean that you forget about your schoolwork. It doesn't mean that you no longer have any time for your friends. It doesn't mean that you stop speaking to your family because you're always on the phone with the one you love!

Having a boyfriend or girlfriend is great. It's a great way to learn about another person while also learning a little bit about yourself. Just don't forget about everything and everyone else in your life while you're dating.

And it goes without saying, when you're dating someone, be careful with how you spend your time and how you treat your body. Healthy, safe, and smart is the way to go.

## MYTH:
I got dumped and my life is completely, totally over!

### MYTHBUSTER:
*All of the clichés apply. You* do *need a little time alone. It* is *better to have loved and lost than not loved at all. There* are *other fish in the sea. So take a little time and then move on. Your life is not over. It has completely, totally just begun!*

# Peer pressure:
## There's a time for work and a time for play.

You've already heard a lot about peer pressure and have maybe even experienced it. What you might not know, though, is that when you experience peer pressure in high school it's rarely in the overly pushy, overly dangerous way that it's presented in assemblies and movies. Instead, you'll have a conversation with a friend who's trying to convince you to close your book and come to the cafeteria. And your friend will be smiling and as friendly as can be as he or she invites you along. Or, perhaps it's your brother or sister telling you to skip your homework because there's a good movie on TV.

So it won't necessarily be a drug dealer lurking at the bus stop or someone trying to convince you to join a cult. It will probably be someone you care about and who cares about you. As long as you recognize that there's a time for work and a time for play, you'll be fine. The nice thing about peer pressure is that sometimes you can give in to it. If you read ahead in your textbook, you can join your brother to watch that movie. If you've studied for that quiz, you can go to the cafeteria for a snack. Luck, they say, is preparation-meet-opportunity, so be lucky when this innocent kind of peer pressure comes your way. And be smart when the not-so-innocent kind comes along.

## "Is there anything I can do to get my work done and have fun?"

*The answer is YES. Your daily planner isn't just for homework, after all. By being aware of upcoming events (plays, pizza, parties) you can get your work done and have fun!*

# Get ready because boys and girls *are* treated differently.

Yes, just as you already know about peer pressure, you are probably aware that there's a difference between girls and boys and the way they are treated by members of the opposite sex. But the purpose of this tip is to prepare you for the different ways in which boys and girls—young men and women now—will be treated when they begin their freshman year. One of the harsh realities of high school is that the freshmen girls will get a lot of attention from the older boys, while the freshmen boys will go through their first year virtually ignored. By everyone!

This is not to say that the girls have it better than the boys. There are pros and cons to each situation.

## Girls

**Pros:** attention, invitations to parties, asked out on dates and/or to the prom, extra help with school work and hints about teachers and tests, etc.

**Cons:** peer pressure, unwanted attention, distractions from schoolwork, risk of rumors or a bad reputation, knowing that with each passing year the boys will pay less and less attention to you as each new class of girls enters the high school.

## Boys

**Cons:** feeling dorky, feeling like you never get invited anywhere, not having any dates, etc.

**Pros:** less peer pressure, fun with your fellow freshmen friends, ability to focus more on schoolwork, knowing that soon your freshman year will end!

# Attending parties, throwing parties.

Most people like to go to parties. High school parties rarely look like the wild affairs seen in the movies, but there are definitely times when things get out of control. This is something you have to be aware of when deciding whether or not to go to a certain party. It's something you have to be superaware of when deciding to throw a party and what kind of party it will be.

Even if you have a party while your parents are home, it can be a pretty stressful experience. You'll worry about whether or not people will even come to your party, and if they do, whether or not your guests will have a good time! The stakes are raised even higher when your parents go out and you try and throw a party without their knowing about it. To state the obvious, this is *not* recommended. For one, there are legal risks. Plus, as was stated in tip #37, earning (and keeping) Mom and Dad's trust is one of the keys to a happy, successful high school experience.

Similarly, you have to keep the potential hazards in mind when deciding about the parties you will or will not attend. If the police show up, are you at risk of getting arrested? What will your parents say? How long will you be grounded? You might get punished even if you don't get arrested.

At least once during high school, you'll be at a party, and the little voice in your head will ask you if you're doing the right thing. Don't worry too much. Just be smart about how long you stay and be smart about what you share with Mom and Dad the next day. Just as there's a lot to be said for avoiding peer pressure, there's a lot to be said for being honest with your parents. There's also a lot to be said for having a good time without putting yourself in harm's way.

# Know the difference between hanging out and loitering.

Every town has a couple of hot spots where kids like to hang out. What are the best places in your town for hanging with your friends? What do they *all* have in common? Usually, one thing: you can chill without getting hassled by adults. No dirty looks and no mention of "Don't you have homework you should be doing?" Nobody comes around to bother you, and that's good news for you and your friends.

So let that be the rule for determining where you hang out. Why go to a spot where there are adults constantly asking you questions or telling you to leave? Go somewhere that's safe and hassle free. It is possible to have fun with your friends, away from your parents, without being a nuisance to store owners and youth officers.

### "What does a hassle-free hangout look like?"

- Well-lit
- Has places to sit
- Has a garbage can nearby so you don't leave a mess
- Has adults nearby, just in case of emergency
- Not on a busy road
- Not blocking people from entering and leaving a place of business
- Not near an area where there's crime

# Try to moderate your use of fun technology.

When it comes to deciding how often to use all of your gadgets, moderation is the best bet. There are cell phones, of course, for talking or text messaging. There's the computer for those who want to e-mail and instant message. Video games are quite possibly the most distracting of all. These are dangerous because they're so much fun. All too easily, one hour can turn into three hours, and the next thing you know, it's midnight and you haven't opened a book yet! That's why, as best you can, you need to limit yourself.

# Hints to Help You Be Disciplined with Technology:

- Turn the computer OFF unless you need it to do your homework.

- Turn your cell phone OFF and just check messages once an hour (and only if you're *expecting* a call).

- Don't touch your video games until all of your homework is done.

- Ask a family member to help you if you're struggling.

```
Moderation (noun):
Restraint or regulation.
```

# Decide how you're going to deal with gossip.

First things first, don't *be* a gossip. Just remember how you'd feel if people were talking about you behind your back. And imagine how you'll feel if you get called out for gossiping. Most of the time, people gossip to impress a potential friend. If that's what it takes to earn this friendship, though, is it really worth it? Remember that the friends you're earning might not be worth the bridges you're burning.

Next, don't let yourself be the victim of gossip. This is a more serious problem, because this situation is less under your control. That's why gossip bothers people so much: they feel like there's nothing they can do about it. Pretty much the only thing you can do is (1) be careful about whom you share your secrets with and (2) clear up an issue as soon as possible, especially if the gossip isn't true. You definitely don't want to just sit back and hope it'll go away.

Sometimes the gossip isn't completely false. If you've made a mistake and people are talking about it, be sure to take responsibility for your actions and try to set things right as soon as possible. Gossip feeds off of exaggeration, so if you let the talkers do their talking, the next thing you know, it won't be that you dumped your boyfriend or girlfriend: it'll be that you threw a rock through their bedroom window with a note attached that read "I hate you and I never...." Just do what you can to put the truth out there.

Finally, there are times that things go too far and the talk becomes threatening. School officials are very well versed in sexual harassment and bullying and know to treat it differently than simple gossip. It's become a legal issue, and school districts can be sued if they don't respond to a student's concerns, so it's worth your while to let a teacher or administrator know. Sometimes, this is the only way that it will ever stop.

# Avoid the drama without acting aloof.

Here are three different paths leading to the same place. It's a place where you rarely, if ever, get caught up in the "he said, she said," where you're able to put your energies into productive activities (homework, sports, friendships, etc.) rather than negative activities (rumors, fighting, etc.), and where you're able to stand apart from the crowd while still being accepted *by* the crowd.

## Path #1

This is the path of least resistance and can be categorized as the "mind your own business" path. It's the path where you find the fewest friends but also the least amount of trouble.

```
Aloof (adjective):
Unfriendly and disinterested.
```

## Path #2

This is a path of minimal resistance and can be categorized as the "good excuse" path. The good excuses can take two forms. The first is when you always come up with a good excuse to get out of a gossipy conversation. For example, "Sorry, my mom's calling me. Gotta go!" The second kind of good excuse is the kind you make for those people who are being talked about: "I don't know why she's acting that way, but there's got to be something else going on. Why don't you ask her?" In this case, you try to direct the conversation in a more positive direction, and by being sympathetic you avoid seeming aloof.

## Path #3

This is the path of most resistance but definitely will keep people from thinking you're a snob. Categorized as "the fixer," this is when you make a suggestion for solving the problem but then leave it up to the people directly involved to work it out on their own. It's like when there are two countries at war and they both ask the United States for help. Our president makes a suggestion for achieving peace and maybe even sets up a meeting for the two sides, but doesn't get any more involved than that. This isn't quite avoiding the drama, but you're not getting all caught up in it, either. And that's a good thing!

# Decide which friends to listen to.

When in need of advice, it's important to have at least one confidant. This isn't just a best friend; this is someone you can use as a sounding board. This is someone whose opinion you can trust.

Like a sage sitting atop a mountain (but much easier to find!), this is the person who can tell you what is the right thing to do and what is the wrong thing; but even more importantly, they won't just give you the easy advice. They won't blow off your problem, share a cliché with you, and then run off to class. You know that you can count on them when in need of help.

If there's just one sage at the top, there are a hundred fools at the base of the mountain. And as hard as it should be to gain your trust, when one of these people takes advantage of it, then it should be hard for them to *re*gain that trust. You have to have confidence in your confidants!

```
Confidant (noun):
A trusted friend.
```

# Proceed with confidence.

Speaking of confidence, the best thing you can do as you make your way through high school is to make your way with confidence. Not cockiness, self-confidence. There are five key areas in which you can demonstrate this belief in yourself.

**Five Key Areas in Which You Can Demonstrate Confidence:**

1.  Carve out your own niche by pursuing your interests and finding other people (students *and* teachers) who share those interests. These areas might include clubs, sports, a job, and/or volunteer work.

2. Be yourself without being a loner by
(a) never acting in a way that goes
against your morals and values and
(b) putting time into those relationships that
are healthy and productive. This area, as with
the other three remaining areas, is social and
involves your friends.

3. Never turn your back on somebody just because
helping out that person is the unpopular thing to
do. This area is also social but involves more
than those people you consider your friends.

   *Read* To Kill a Mockingbird *for a great example of this:
   the main character's father, Atticus Finch, is a lawyer
   who defends a black man even though many people in
   the town think he's guilty and doesn't deserve defense.*

4. Don't get sucked into friendships/situations
just to be popular.

5. When you're willing to make unexpected friends
in unexpected places, this is a real sign that
you're a confident person.

   *It's worth mentioning that this is also the number-one
   way to fight against having too many cliques in your
   school or at least in your class.*

# Break down the walls between cliques.

### Sample Cliques

- ✓ Cheerleaders
- ✓ Gangstas
- ✓ Geeks
- ✓ Goths
- ✓ Jocks
- ✓ Metal Heads
- ✓ Preps

There are some hurtful names in that list, and your first step in breaking down the walls between the cliques is to *not* use any of them.

**Q:** "Why should I bother trying to be friends with people in other cliques?"

**A:** *The better question is "Why not?" These are people whose company you might just enjoy, whom you might have a lot in common with, and from whom you might learn a lot. Besides, they might be judging you on your looks or who your friends are, and wouldn't it be nice to let them get to really know you?*

The best place to make friends with people who seem different than you is in the classroom. It's one of the many—yes, many—things that you have in common. It might be tough to start up a conversation in the cafeteria or some other central place, but in class there's plenty to talk about and people tend to be by themselves or with just one or two friends.

# Surviving "Freshman Fridays."

Not every school has a tradition like "Freshman Fridays" and hopefully your school doesn't either, but there's liable to be some sort of traditional, unofficial hazing day where the freshmen are the target. If it's all in good fun, then you really don't have much to worry about, but if you've heard some scary stories about "Freshman Fridays" of the past, then heed the following advice:

1. Lay low at lunchtime (maybe even eat in a classroom with a teacher).

2. Avoid those hallways where most of the action takes place. This includes avoiding the temptation to go check out those hallways to see what's happening.

**3.** Don't draw unnecessary attention to yourself, thus becoming a frequent target. Upperclassmen will target cocky freshmen, so be humble, be cool, and be quiet!

## Some Potential "Freshman Friday" Pranks:

- Getting locked in a locker
- Getting stuffed into a garbage can
- Wedgies
- Stolen textbooks
- "Kick Me" sign or shaving cream on the back
- Water guns and water balloons
- Bullying and/or harassment (this should be reported to the school's administrators or a teacher immediately)

# TIP 82

# See for yourself that not all upper-classmen are evil!

High school is fun, and it *will* be fun for you. There are plenty of nice kids in your school, both in your class and in the upper grades. Some will approach you, but more often than not, you'll have to make the first effort. Do so. It's worth it!

Conform (verb):

Do the accepted thing; be consistent with the actions of others.

## Benefits of Befriending Upperclassmen:

- They'll have their own list of helpful hints for you.
- You may receive invitations to fun events that most freshmen don't get invited to.
- Having one friend always leads to making other new friends.
- They can drive and might be able to give you rides.

At the same time that you're seeking out those nonevil upperclassmen, take it upon yourself to prove to the older kids that not all freshmen are immature. Avoid the cockiness mentioned in the previous tip and let humility be just one of the mature characteristics that you exhibit. This is one time it's okay to conform a bit and just go with the flow. Be friendly. That's all.

# **83**

# **Get yourself out of a dangerous car.**

There is a bad side to having a good social life. For example, every once in a while you'll be in a situation that makes you uncomfortable. And believe it or not, this can be a good thing for you—in the long run. It's a good experience to go through, like a real-life test to see how you handle yourself. In the case of getting into a car when you shouldn't, it's a test you really must pass.

Whether the driver is just a bit wild, driving at unnecessarily high speeds, or has had too much to drink, it's absolutely, positively the 100 percent truth that your parents would rather have you call them for a ride than receive a call from the police after an accident. The worst that can happen if you call your parents is that you will get punished because you were out past curfew or somewhere you weren't supposed to be. Beats getting injured in an accident, doesn't it?

Some towns/schools have a Drug Abuse Resistance Education, Mothers Against Drunk Driving, or Safe Rides program. You can count on them too. If your school doesn't have one, consider starting it. Tip #53 describes how to recruit members and an advisor, so revisit that for further advice. The only additional resource you'll need is a place to house the program on Friday and Saturday nights. Fortunately, many organizations (The Boys and Girls Club, for example) will be willing to give you the necessary space.

## Looking to the Future

*Keep in mind that you want to build a lot of trust with your parents before you become a driver. If your family has enough money, your parents might consider buying you a car. Making good choices during your freshman and sophomore years can help to convince them that you can handle the responsibility.*

# Share a smile, save a life.

It's worth it to try to help someone when they look down and out. Often, all it takes is a smile and some kind words, but there are other times when you might need to give a little more.

Although the first, nervous instinct might be just to let the person be, if you see a friend or acquaintance that seems really down about something, reach out to them. In turn, if it seems like serious trouble is brewing, consult an adult. This should happen even if it means breaking that friend's trust. It's important for their well-being, and you don't want to risk having to live with guilt should some harm come to that person.

In those situations where sharing a smile isn't enough, you might end up saving a life. This is a reality that you'll encounter more and more as you grow up. Don't hesitate to open the phone book or call the police to learn about the most relevant hotline or help line.

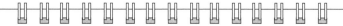

## Problems That Some High School Students Experience:

- Anger management
- Anorexia and/or bulimia
- Depression
- Drugs
- Physical abuse
- Sexual issues including diseases and pregnancy

# Keep things in perspective.

Whether you're experiencing a high or a low, the important thing is that you stay calm and put the situation into perspective. You should, to the best of your ability, look at the big picture. For example, if you had an overall average of 92 percent in your math class but received a 70 percent on a quiz, rather than being overly upset about that score, take solace in the fact that your quarterly grade will still be a 90 percent.

On the other hand, if you lead your team to victory, get the highest grade on an art project, or win a trillion dollars in the lottery, don't lose your mind with excitement. Smile, sit down, be happy, and don't act like an idiot! People don't like to hang out with idiots. Don't get too high on the highs and don't get too low on the lows. You'll be better off that way.

## Some of the Low Points You Might Experience in High School:

- Low test score or quarterly grade
- Getting in trouble with parents and/or school officials and/or the police
- Having a fight
- Experiencing the end of a friendship
- Being dumped
- Hearing that there's a rumor going around school about you
- Having someone close to you pass away
- Getting rejected by a college

## Some of the High Points You Might Experience in High School:

- Academic achievement
- Athletic achievement
- Making a new good friend
- Somebody you care about tells you they love you
- First paycheck
- Getting into the college of your choice

# Monitor yourself.

To one degree or another, you'll have to get better and better at monitoring yourself as you make your way through high school. Even students with highly involved parents must learn how to create their own schedules to get all of their work done. In the middle, there are those students whose parents are interested but not really involved.

Clearly, these kids have to monitor their schedule on their own and make whatever changes are necessary. The last group of students is the group that seems (to some of their peers) to have it the best but actually has it the worst. These are the kids whose parents just don't care at all. It's most important that they keep themselves in check, monitoring their performance and progress the way a caring parent would.

## Beware! Beware! Beware!

*There are times when a teenager from any of the three aforementioned groups has the opportunity to "get away with it." The following are examples of opportunities to get away with something—and the potential repercussions:*

1. **The science teacher has to step out into the hall during a quiz and you get three of the five answers from a friend, enabling you to pass the quiz.**

   *Then, because you never learned the material covered on that quiz, you get those questions wrong on the midterm exam and fail it!*

2. **There's a huge party, and because your parents are going to be out all night, you take their car (even though you don't have a license yet), pick up a friend, and go.**

   *Not only do the police break up the party, but they also stop each car on the way out to check licenses and you get arrested.*

3. **Both of your parents got promotions at work and now don't get home until after dinner, so they no longer check to make sure you've done your homework. On some nights, you skip doing it, and nobody seems to notice.**

   *Your parents didn't notice, but three of your teachers did and they tell Mom and Dad all about it at parent-teacher conferences.*

# Take good care of yourself.

If you learn just one thing from this book, learn this: **you're the only *you* you've got!**

The point of this is that you need to take care of that only *you*. You need to respect your body and the gift of life that you've been given. The goal is to live as long as you can and as happily and as healthily as you can.

So in addition to being very wary of the dangers of drinking and drugs, also know that having bad eating habits can do you major harm. In turn, it's important to have good sleeping habits. Yes, you've got to work hard; yes, you should go out with your friends and have fun; but no, you should not put yourself at risk by getting just a couple of hours of sleep, by eating junk food all the time, and by partying too hard.

## The Basics of Good Health Checklist:

✓ Get lots of sleep.

✓ Eat lots of fruits and vegetables to support you through your growth spurts.

✓ Don't put any poisons into your body. Remember it this way: "No CAD," which means "No Cigarettes, Alcohol, or Drugs"

✓ Find the balance between obesity and anorexia; easier said than done, but you can do it! Besides, it's important to form good habits now, because it will be harder to break bad habits later.

✓ Avoid potentially violent or destructive situations.

# PART SEVEN

# Family.

# Stay in touch with your family.

Not necessarily *you,* but many teenagers have a tendency to put their families last on the list of priorities. Everything from going to the movies to napping comes before hanging out with Mom and Dad and your siblings. Some high school students think it's not cool to be seen with the family. They walk way ahead of them when they all go out together. Or they walk way behind. Kind of silly, don't you think?

First of all, your family really isn't *that* bad. They did raise you, and they do love you. Besides, every single student at your school has a family, so if somebody sees you with your family, they aren't going to think that you're an alien or freak. They might think you're not having as much fun as they are at the moment, but it really won't ruin your reputation.

There's also this to consider: long after all of those other kids are gone from your life, your family will still be around. And to further the point, do you really want to disrespect people you're going to need someday? This applies to extended family, as well. Be nice to Grandma and Grandpa. Take time to hang out with your cousins. Visit your aunts and uncles. They need you, and you need them. They like you, and if you think about it, you like them too!

## Family as a Resource

*Keep in mind that all of the older family members were freshmen once too. Why not use them as a resource? When you have a question about studying, surviving a breakup, or deciding what to do about a job, you can usually count on family members for honest answers.*

# Keep up with family traditions.

### Top Five Family Traditions:

1. Holiday celebrations
2. Sunday night dinner with the extended family
3. Religious celebrations
4. Attending sporting events
5. Movie night, minigolf, amusement park, etc.

Just because you're a teenager now doesn't mean you can skip out on the family, especially when it comes to traditional events and celebrations. Being grown up now certainly doesn't exclude you, considering that all of the older folks in your family attend, right? Even if what your family likes to do seems corny, it's important to them and it should be *important* to you too.

Believe it or not, someday you will actually feel nostalgic for these family get-togethers. Sometimes, traditions fade out as people move away or, unfortunately, pass away. The traditions are a part of your childhood memories, and you'll find yourself missing them. You may even try and revive them when you become a father or mother!

Hanging out at the coffee shop with your friends is, without a doubt, more fun than going to Grandma's house for your aunt's birthday, but your aunt once changed your diapers, and she'll be sitting there with a big, proud smile on her face when you graduate. Buy her a present, write a nice card, and be there when she blows out the candles.

```
Nostalgic (adjective):

Longing or reminiscent; looking
back fondly.
```

# TIP 90

# Don't treat your house like a hotel.

| Yes or No? | | |
|---|---|---|
| 1. Do you ever do your own laundry? | ☐ Yes | ☐ No |
| 2. Do you ever help cook dinner? | ☐ Yes | ☐ No |
| 3. Do you ever wash dishes or load the dishwasher? | ☐ Yes | ☐ No |
| 4. Do you ever take the garbage out? | ☐ Yes | ☐ No |
| 5. Do you ever dust? Vacuum? Clean windows? | ☐ Yes | ☐ No |

If you answered no to more than two of the above questions, then look up the word *evict* in the dictionary, because your parents are about to evict you! Your house doesn't look like a hotel. Your father doesn't stand by the kitchen counter waiting for a bell to ring so he can serve you. Your mother doesn't push a cart from room to room, calling out, "Housecleaning!" Maybe sometimes you want to treat your house like a hotel, and maybe sometimes you think of Dad as your bellhop and Mom as a maid, but don't make that mistake. It's one of the most disrespectful (and annoying) things you can do.

Your parents won't appreciate it if you never, ever help around the house. And they'll definitely get ticked off if you're constantly making a mess and leaving it for them to clean up. If you want their respect, give them the respect they deserve. Hang out with your family when you're at home, rather than constantly coming and going, and chip in as part of the team.

```
Evict (verb):
Throw out, expel, force to leave.
```

# Avoid the drama with your mama!

As a teenager, there will be many times that you find yourself at odds with your parents. They'll feel one way about something, and you'll feel another. You'll want something, and they, for whatever reason, won't or can't give it to you. But because you want it so bad, you might have a hard time understanding why. Just do the best you can to avoid the drama.

The important thing for you to understand is that it's extremely exhausting for your parents to have to argue with you. There's nothing wrong with trying to rephrase your request or maybe make a compromise, but after you hear no for the second or third time, your best bet is to just let it go. If you don't, if this little conversation all of a sudden blows up into an argument, then you're making a big deal out of a small problem.

## Small Problems That Have Potential to be Big Deals:

- Getting grounded
- Getting questioned about low grades
- Being asked to stay in one night to help out (to babysit, do chores, spend time with your family, etc.)
- Hearing that your parents are disappointed in the choices you're making
- Hearing that your parents can't lend you the money you need

Someday, you'll laugh about your teenage years with your parents. You'll admit to being irrational at times, and your folks will admit that they probably should have trusted you a little bit more. It will be harder to laugh about those years if every issue is turned into a fight. Do all you can to try to get what you want without being nasty, because nasty behavior leaves people with really bad memories.

# Remember your younger siblings.

For those of you lucky enough to have siblings, this is another relationship that deserves your attention throughout the high school years. It's especially important if you have a younger sibling or siblings.

You might not believe it, but those little kids running around the house, smearing food on your stuff and yelling in your unoccupied ear when you're trying to talk on the phone, really look up to you. Anytime you pay attention to them, they glow for hours afterwards. They remember every move you make and mimic it as soon as the opportunity presents itself—from small things like how you dress to big things like how you talk to your parents.

So it's important to their future that you set as good an example as possible. There's also the idea of contributing to their growth. Every kid deserves to have a great childhood, and with just the occasional small effort, here and there, you can give your brothers and sisters something to smile about.

## "What can I do with a little kid?"

1. *Read them a book, comic book, newspaper, or magazine*
2. *Watch a movie*
3. *Ask about school: friends? hardest subject? favorite lunch? any fun field trips?*
4. *Go somewhere: ice cream shop, library, park, etc.*
5. *Play board games, video games, and sports*
6. *Cook a meal*
7. *Go shopping*

# Invite your parents to visit your school.

Invite your parents in to show them around the school. This will probably be sometime after school as one, if not both, of your parents work. But the time doesn't really matter. The point is simply to show them around and give them a feel for what high school is like today.

**Cons:**

- Your parents will be in your school.
- Other kids might see you . . . with your parents . . . in your school!

**Pros:**

- Your parents will better understand your world.
- Your parents will better understand that you have a life of your own.
- Your parents might get to meet some of your friends, and that always builds trust.
- Your parents will appreciate that you're sharing part of your life with them.

Inviting your parents in to see your school is a very mature thing to do, and it really is true that little efforts like this go a long way toward building a good relationship with Mom and Dad. Plus, it might be fun!

# Form a friendship with your folks.

The older you get, the smaller the generation gap will seem between you and your parents. You will someday graduate and enter the world of work, and all of a sudden, your world won't be that different from Mom and Dad's world. That's because, like Mom and Dad, you're now an adult!

Parents are advice givers. They are trusted sources of information. They are a shoulder to lean on and a safe haven when the world is getting you down. They like to enjoy themselves, and they enjoy your company. In a nutshell, your parents will always be your parents, but as you get older, they can actually become your friends. And as with all friendships, the benefits go both ways: for them *and* for you.

So as you slowly work your way out of being dependent on them and closer to being friends with them, learn about their world and let them learn about yours. Keep their needs and feelings in mind, and they're sure to do the same for you.

## MYTH:
"My parents just don't understand!"

### MYTHBUSTER:

*Your parents* do *understand because they were once in high school too. It's just hard for them to remember what it's like because they are so busy. So help Mom and Dad out; give them a reminder of what life is like in high school.*

# PART EIGHT

# Looking ahead: College, the military, and the world of work.

# Determine your goals.

**"What is a goal?"**

A goal is an ambition that you have. It's a target that you aim for. It's a purpose that drives what you do.

**"Why should I have goals?"**

People are at their best when they have a purpose. When there's a reason for working hard every day, then a sense of satisfaction can be achieved.

**"How should I determine my goals?"**

You should have three goals for yourself. (It's OK to change the goals.) You should decide on a short-term goal for the next three months, a midterm goal for the next year, and a long-term goal for you to achieve by the time you graduate high school.

One example of a short-term goal is raising your English grade from the 79 percent you earned first quarter to an 85 percent in the second quarter. One example of a midterm goal is saving $250 by summer vacation so that you can go on a canoe trip. One example of a long-term goal is earning a varsity letter in tennis.

These goals shouldn't just be in your head, either. If you remember some of the tips from the first section of this book, then you know that visual reminders are always a good idea. Jot your goals down and put the piece of paper someplace where you will see it every day.

# Refer to your references!

You probably don't have any references yet. You might not even know what a reference is. Well, no big deal! By figuring all of this out before applying for your first job, you'll be well ahead of the game.

---

**Reference (noun):**

A person who provides a good recommendation.

NOTE: The word *reference* can also be used to describe the letter that someone writes for you. Some colleges and jobs request these letters.

Your potential references include, as you would expect, your teachers and guidance counselor, but don't forget any employers, coaches, and club advisors you know. Do whatever it takes to impress them, because when the time comes for a reference, you want that adult to be able to speak so highly of you that there's no doubt in the mind of the person who inquired about you. Whether that person is the director of a program you're hoping will accept you, a potential employer, or a college admissions counselor, you want that person to think that you're the greatest. You want that person to *want* to get to know you as your reference knows you.

You don't want to have to ask virtual strangers to give you a reference. Some adults will do it for you, just because they feel bad for you, but most will simply say that they don't know you well enough and don't feel comfortable recommending you. Save yourself from that embarrassment.

# Seek employment that offers more than just a paycheck.

These are many ways that a job can offer you more than money. Tip #67 focused on the pros of an internship, the main benefits being experience and earning yourself a reference from a person working in a field of your interest. Experience goes a long way toward your education, just as a reference goes a long way toward opening doors for the future. At the heart of this tip, though, is the idea of getting a job that you truly love. It's very,

very hard to get motivated for work if you have no interest in the work you're doing. And there are many jobs for teenagers that offer very little interest or enjoyment. You're scooping ice cream. You're changing diapers. You're mopping a floor or cleaning candy wrappers out from between movie seats. All of these jobs pay, but do they have anything to do with a potential career?

In addition to giving you some experience and a couple of bucks, some jobs and internships give you the opportunity to serve people in need. This is similar to volunteer work but with more potential for possible employment after college. Working in a hospital or rehabilitation facility, reading with younger children, or helping to run fundraisers allows you to earn a paycheck while giving back to society.

# Seek an advisor.

Once you make a connection with an adult, try to follow up once a week by stopping in to say hi. Let the relationship grow so that this person can become an advisor to you. You'll have a trusted source for advice *and* somebody who'll be willing to recommend you when called upon for a reference.

Whether it's your teacher (stop in to say hi during office hours or after school help) or guidance counselor, you can benefit from the relationship by being a fully engaged, participating member of the partnership. In today's busy world, though, the student has to create opportunities to meet with this advisor. Why? Because the student benefits more than the adult from the relationship, so with that greater interest comes the greater responsibility. Plus, adults are super busy, especially the ones that kids like and trust.

Keep in mind that whether this advisor is a teacher, guidance counselor, coach, or boss, when you need something, try to avoid making it a last-minute demand. Not only is this rude, you might find yourself out in the cold if the adult is too busy. Remember that an emergency for you is not necessarily an emergency for them.

# Pick your path rather than having it picked for you.

In Robert Frost's poem, "The Road Not Taken," the subject of the poem decides to go down the path that grabbed his interest rather than simply taking the path that everyone else had chosen. The poem might be familiar to you because it's so often referred to, especially regarding young adults. This is because people your age have to make so many important decisions about what they will do with their life.

But the road less traveled is not always the right road for you. What really matters is that you put some thought into your decision. Athletes visualize their actions before taking a shot or swing. They call on their imagination to see things through before making their first move. You have to do the same when deciding whether to take honors classes or not, whether you'll try out for the team, whether sneaking out of the house is a good idea, whether you'll work over the summer or go to camp, whether you'll have that beer or say "No thanks, I'm driving," whether you'll ask so-and-so to the dance or go with your friends.

Just about every decision in high school seems life changing, but that's OK. If you take every decision seriously, then you'll be willing to put some thought into the path you pick. And the more thoughtfulness you show, the more willing people will be to let you choose your own road; and as a teenager, do you want other people making your decisions for you?

# Have a plan.

Advising you to look before you leap and to carefully choose the road you will travel are two ways of saying that you should have a plan. Anytime you think before acting, anytime you map out ahead of time how you'll proceed, you're being wise.

You can practice having a plan. In every little thing you do, if you think about the steps you're going to follow, you're getting yourself prepared for those bigger, more important decisions. One benefit to forming a plan ahead of time is you give yourself the chance to prepare for the inevitable disappointment. Disappointments happen, so do yourself a favor and come up with a Plan B. When you think of the B in Plan B, think of *backup* because a Plan B plan is a backup plan. It's your way of rolling with the punches so that you can move on.

## Three Examples of How a Plan B Can Help:

1. If you lose the election for class president, your Plan B could be running for class representative.

2. If you don't make the varsity team, your Plan B could be asking the coach for a spot on the junior varsity.

3. If your parents say no about going to the big party Friday night, your Plan B could be a little party at your place. (Other people will, undoubtedly, not be allowed to go either, so why not?)

Whatever it is you're doing or trying to do, always remember to have a backup plan so that a bump in the road doesn't completely throw you off track. And the better your Plan B is, the better you will be able to handle those disappointments.

# Discussing your next step.

Everything you do in high school is in preparation for your next step. Whether it's going to college, getting a job, or joining the military, there are going to be people you care about who agree with that next step and others who disagree.

Although you'll be feeling overwhelmed as you prepare for this next step, try to take the time to talk to the special people in your life about what you're doing and why. They might not be level headed in their assessment of what you're doing, but that doesn't mean that *you* have to be emotional too. What's really bothering them is that they can't control your next move. This is especially true for people in your family.

In addition to not being able to control your next move, they probably don't like the fact that what's important to them isn't necessarily important to you. But at the heart of the matter is the fact that they care. You should take their worry as a compliment. Listen to what they have to say, see if you can't match their advice with what you really want for yourself, and then explain what you're doing and why. If it isn't good enough for them, well, then it's their problem and not yours. But don't leave them in the past just because of this. Keep in touch and give them reason to be excited about the road you're now traveling. Eventually they'll come around. They love you too much not to!

## About the Author

Randy Howe teaches in New Haven, Connecticut. He has written more than ten books, including *First Year Teacher: What I Wish I'd Known My First 100 Days on the Job* and *Speak to Me: Great American Texts Demystified for Today's Text-Messaging Students*.